Hey God, Are We There Yet?

The Rewards of Waiting on God

GOD AT WORK

Yet those who wait for the Lord
Will gain new strength;
They will mount up with wings like eagles,
They will run and not get tired,
They will walk and not become weary.
Isaiah 40:31

Robert John Morrissette

Hey God, Are We There Yet?
Author: Robert John Morrissette
ISBN: 978-0976354949
Library of Congress Control Number: 2016900574

Publisher
Big Blue Skies of Idaho, LLC
Coeur d'Alene, Idaho 83815
United States of America

Bible Versions Information
New International Version® (NIV) Copyright ©1973 by
    International Bible Society
New American Standard Bible® Copyright © 1995 by The
    Lockman Foundation
The Message (MSG) Copyright © 2002
King James Version (KJV) No copyright: public domain

Edited by: Mark Sandford
Cover and layout design by: Robert John Morrissette
Printed by: CreateSpace, Charleston, SC, USA

Unless otherwise stated, all verses quoted throughout this book are from the New American Standard Bible.

Note: As appropriate, names and other identifying information used throughout this book as illustrations have been changed to protect privacy.

May the Lord give you courage, strength and grace
during your seasons of waiting,
as you persevere and endure by faith in Him
for the amazing things He has in store for you!
And may you finish well!

About the Author

Rob's experiences include being a prayer minister, professional counselor, software engineer, automotive R&D technician, author, publisher, teacher and speaker. His desire is for others to experience the Father's love.

For information about prayer ministry...

EH

elijah house
healing hearts. changing lives.

Elijah House is an international Christian prayer-ministry organization with locations throughout the world.

Elijah House provides:
- Teaching and training: schools and seminars
- Resources: books, DVDs and CDs
- Prayer ministry and internships

To locate an Elijah House near you...
Go to: ElijahHouse.org

Scan code below to go to website.

Other Books by Rob Morrissette

Pray Through It: How to identify and resolve problems that are rooted in unresolved issues from your past. This book contains applications and many encouraging stories of those who experienced change. ISBN: 978-0976354963
(Also available in Spanish: *Oraciòn que toca las racìces* ISBN: 978-0976354918)

Generational Restoration: How to identify and resolve generational issues. Discover God's plan for restoring the generations, and how you can be the one He can use to help do it! ISBN: 978-0976354970

**God is good,
All the time!**

Contents

Waiting

There is a time for everything,
and a season for every activity under the heavens.
...He has made everything beautiful in its time.
Ecclesiastics 3:1, 11^{NIV}

A good friend once said, "Most of life is about waiting." The longer I live, the more I see how true this is.

From the day we were conceived to the day we pass from this life, waiting plays a definite role in everything we do. Whether it is our plans, decisions or relationships, waiting is always involved in one form or another.

While anticipating our arrival, people waited for us to be born. As a baby, when we were hungry, we had to wait for someone to respond to our cry. While waiting for Christmas, it seemed so far away, yet so wonderful when it finally arrived. We could hardly wait until our tooth fell out or when we would grow one inch taller. Whether it was waiting for our father because he had been away on a long trip or because we had gotten into trouble while he was at work, either way it felt like an eternity!

And then there's that long list of times when we said, "I can't wait until..." Just fill in the blank. "I can't wait until I grow up." "I can't wait until we go on vacation." "I can't wait until I get my driver's license." While children often say, "I can't wait until school is out," soon after, some parents find themselves saying, "I can't wait until school starts again!"

There are those short-term times of waiting, such as waiting for a phone call, a reply email or a response to a text message. There is waiting in traffic or for a table at a restaurant. We may have been able to place an order via the internet, but we still have to wait for the item to arrive. Even though microwave ovens have sped-up cooking time, we still have to wait for it to finish reheating our coffee.

Then there are those long-term times of waiting. Perhaps we have been waiting for that special someone to come into our life, or we are waiting for that someone already in our life to change. There is waiting for a wound to heal or to get over an illness. We wonder when we will finally have a break or change in our life. Many of us are waiting for the Lord to answer a long-time prayer request.

If you are like me, you don't like to wait. It seems like such an inconvenience. It messes with your plans and interferes with your goals. I have found myself thinking: "What a waste of time! Here I was, finally making some progress, and now there's another delay. This can't be God's will — or is it?!"

Another thing I have discovered about waiting is that most of us are not very good at it. Definitely, waiting is not something we strive to get better at doing. Think about it; who do you know who goes out of their way to improve their waiting skills? And how many people do you think would sign up for a seminar called, "Waiting 101 — Mastering the Art of Waiting (and Other Such Delays)"? If anything, most of us do whatever we can to avoid waiting.

I have also discovered that waiting comes to us — we don't have to go looking for it; it finds us. Throughout our day, it shows up randomly. We find ourselves caught in traffic. We are put on hold while placing an order or calling a doctor. How often, despite how carefully we select a grocery checkout-line, do we still have to wait? When we make our "to-do" list for the day, there is no need to add "waiting" to the list. It will be there as needed. Sure, we can do our best to minimize our contact with waiting. But waiting will still finds a way into our day.

There is a type of waiting that comes by choice. Like when we can make an impulse purchase, but decide to wait and see if we can get a better deal. Or, we decide to sleep on it, to see if it's really what we want to buy. Perhaps we choose to wait to have dessert after we eat dinner. Maybe we agree when someone asks us to save them a seat or a place in line. Or, instead of giving-up on that certain person in our lives who is struggling and lost to us, we choose to still be there for them, waiting to celebrate their eventual return.

Waiting comes in various packages. It can be brief, as in a few seconds to several minutes. Or it can be long, as in months or even years. Sometimes we know how long it will be, but most of the time we don't. Time flies while you're having fun, yet time seems to drag on when you have to wait.

Since waiting is such a regular part of our lives, God must have a special purpose for it. And by the way, He does!

If you look in the Bible, you'll find some interesting insights about waiting. For one, the times people had to wait are mentioned almost as many times as when people were healed. So waiting must be pretty important. Furthermore, God had a unique plan for those who went through times of waiting or were willing to wait. Whether God had them on a short-term waiting plan (hours, days or months) or a many-year-plan, in the end, God did amazing things in and through their lives. Later in this book, we will take a look at many of these examples.

Since waiting is so important in God's economy, let's take a look at what it means to wait.

Here are some thoughts about waiting:
Waiting is what you do while you anticipate what you are seeking. It is hopeful anticipation.

It is enduring the passage of time.

It is a delay from the hustle and bustle of your life.

It is pausing while temporary and apparent obstacles come and go on your journey as you move forward in life.

It is a break from what you consider to be urgent, allowing you to consider that perhaps things are not as pressing as you have assumed, and that God is possibly in control.

It is refusing the urge to quit, even though you have experienced a setback. It is trusting that what appears to be a delay for you is not a delay to the Lord.

It is resisting the temptation to take a shortcut. It is not avoiding the obstacles in front of you, but heading right into them.

It is a gift of a timeout, if you choose it, allowing you a moment to ponder and gain more insight before you begin moving forward again. It is a time when God can show and teach you things you would not be able to learn otherwise.

It is strategic time set aside, to prepare you for what is yet to come.

It is God answering you when you had prayed, "Make me like You, Lord."

It is being faithful in the little ordinary, everyday things. Waiting usually happens during the mundane moments of life.

It is not allowing impatience and a sense of insignificance to rule you while it appears that nothing is happening.

It is the opportunity to learn that you can rest while you wait — that you don't have to put off resting until the waiting is over.

It is the opportunity to see things from God's perspective.

It is resisting the lie that the Lord has somehow forgotten you when it seems that He is working only in the lives of others.

It is a time to choose to not be moved from what you are seeking from the Lord and what He has promised, despite setbacks and delays.

It is anticipating that the glass is on its way from being half-empty to overflowing.

It is a time of preparation for what is about to happen next.

There are no shortcuts when waiting. Time cannot be stored up; it only be spent. So, while you are waiting for this season of waiting to pass, how you spend it is what is important.

Times of waiting are opportunities to take a break to reflect, regroup, and rest. They are gifts to remind us that the Lord is not in a hurry, and that He is in control of time. And therefore, we have no need to be in a hurry.

Time does not "heal all wounds." Time does not change anything. Rather, how you spend your time while you wait, cooperating with God's process in your life — this is what will bring about healing and change.

Waiting upon the Lord is time well invested!

I have found that patience is often associated with waiting. Waiting tests your ability to be patient, and patience helps pass the time while waiting. One of the purposes of waiting is: to teach you patience.

Here are some thoughts about patience:

Patience is the capacity to accept or tolerate delay, trouble, or suffering without getting angry or upset.

It is refusing to let the moment at hand determine your sense of purpose and urgency.

It is recognizing that you will get to where you need to be when the time is right, knowing that the Lord is in charge.

It is knowing and resting in the fact that what is happening at the moment does not change God's goodness and the good things He has in store.

It is the ability to look beyond the storm, knowing that the storm will pass.

It is knowing that you don't have to make a decision right now, even though you feel the pressure to do so.

It is giving time a chance to do its work.

It is the willingness to trust that even though things are not clear right now, they will be, if given enough time.

It is resisting the urge to be like everyone else — upset, frustrated, anxious, etc. — just because things are not going as you had hoped or planned.

It is resisting the urge that you must do something since nothing seems to be happening.

It is remaining calm, no matter what apparent hindrances have been thrown in your way.

It is resting in the tranquility of the Lord, despite the apparent storm around you. It is focusing on and abiding in His peace in the midst of the storm. It is knowing that the sun is still shining, even though there are clouds hiding it from view.

It is living life from God's perspective — He has all the time in the world, and He is not in any hurry.

It is a fruit of the Holy Spirit (Galatians 5:22). Just as the things of the Spirit supersede and transcend things in the natural, learning to walk in the Spirit allows you to rise above your circumstances.

It allows you to give God a chance to work in the midst of your situation, and to see Him do so — which you would have otherwise missed if you had been distracted by impatience.

It is knowing that God is doing something, when it may appear that He is doing nothing.

It is realizing that God is not bound by time, and therefore, what you are going through is not a delay for Him.

It is choosing peace, although your circumstances are telling you there is none.

It is not allowing your circumstances to dictate how you should respond.

It is defying your situation by abiding in peace, even though your circumstances are tempting you to overreact.

It is an opportunity to master waiting instead of letting waiting master you!

In the midst of waiting, patience is a choice. Patience is not allowing the wait to get the best of you. It is doing your best while you wait.

When you are not patient, you miss out on what waiting has in store for you. Impatience is abiding in your circumstances rather than in the Lord. Patience is abiding in the Lord despite your circumstances.

Without recognizing that the Lord is in control, being patient while waiting does not make sense. Waiting is seen only as a hindrance to our goals. Times of waiting become obstacles to avoid and get around. We feel justified in manipulating our circumstances and others in order to bypass the waiting. We seek ways to not wait. Thus, we do whatever it takes to achieve our objective. Our premise becomes: "The end justifies the means." From such a viewpoint, waiting has little or no value.

But in God's economy, waiting is of great value. It is what He uses to build faith by providing opportunities to walk in faith. He also uses waiting to build character into our lives. We tend not to want to wait, for fear that we will miss out on something. In reality, when we don't wait, we miss out on the opportunity to trust God and see Him do great things.

Waiting teaches you:
- Appreciation for what you do have, despite what you don't have.
- Insights about God you would not have learned otherwise.

- That knowing about God's love is not enough, but experiencing His love is.
- That there are things you cannot change about yourself, but God can.
- That you cannot earn what God wants to give you.
- To rely on God, and not on your own strength and abilities. That in order to move forward, you must be dependent upon Him.
- That wherever you are, as difficult as it might be, your difficulties don't have to control you.
- To focus on the Lord and not on your circumstances.
- That at any time, the Lord can change your situation.
- That God's goal is not to remove the present obstacles in your life, but to teach that you can overcome despite them. The Lord uses those very obstacles to make you into who you need to be.
- That you are not in control, but He is — and that He can do amazing things!

Waiting accomplishes the following:
- Reveals areas in your heart that only God can change.
- Removes useless distractions from your life.
- Reinforces your faith as you exercise trust.
- Rids you of unnecessary cares — cares that normally consume, control and drive you. Such cares cause you to forget what really matters.
- Restores your focus on what really matters — the Lord and His purposes.

Waiting is not about doing nothing. It is about what you do while you wait that matters. So, while waiting, don't let what you are not able to do distract you from what you can do. Make the most of what you can do!

The Purpose of Waiting
There are many profound reasons why the Lord has people go through long times of waiting. Almost always, it is obscured and unknown to the one who is waiting. During such times there are

often frustrations, confusion, and struggles with doubt: "What was I thinking?" or "Did I do something wrong?" There is the temptation to quit and to question one's faith. We might even be inclined to question God: "Where are You, God?" "Why are You being so mean to me?" Or, "Why me?"

In the midst of waiting, you may have no idea how the waiting is making any difference. But it is. And it will. In most instances, this is revealed only when the waiting is over. The result will not only affect your life, but the lives of others. What you overcome, you will someday help someone else get through. It will give them that extra boost to get back up, try again, and endure to the end.

Later in this book we will take a look at God's purposes for waiting, in the lives of many individuals. You will be encouraged that the Lord has a purpose for your times of waiting.

The Overall Purpose of Enduring Times of Waiting

God always has a unique purpose He wants to accomplish by having us endure times of waiting. As we will see later in this book, whenever God has us wait, He has the following in mind:

- To prepare us for His intended purpose — to build character.
- To give us an opportunity to believe Him for who He is, despite all our obstacles and impossibilities — to increase our faith.
- To give us what we were really seeking — to reward our faith.
- …And when our time of waiting is over, to allow us the privilege to encourage others during their times of waiting — so they can bear good fruit.

Waiting on the Lord is worth it!

Application
- Why do you find it so hard to wait?
- Recall a time when you had to wait. What challenges did you have to face?
- In what ways have you been tempted to avoid waiting?
- What have you learned from waiting?
- What will you do differently the next time you are faced with a time of waiting?

Faith

Now faith is the assurance of things hoped for,
the conviction of things not seen.
For by it the men of old gained approval...
And without faith it is impossible to please Him,
for he who comes to God must believe that He is,
and that He is a rewarder of those who seek Him.
Hebrews 11:1-2, 6

Walking by Faith

For no apparent reason a strange thing happened to my bother-in-law, Mike. He began having non-remitting headaches, sometimes spiking to excruciating levels. He tried dealing with it through prayer, yet with no-avail. He attempted getting medical help. He went to three different neurologists, took shots and pills, and even had therapy. And still, it made no difference. His condition caused him to lose his natural sense of motivation. His feelings went flat. He lost his usual sense purpose and passion. He soon found himself having to consciously choose to motivate himself.

As a pastor, Mike found this experience to be especially challenging. He no longer felt God's direction or presence. Instead of waking up each day with a sense of direction, he had to choose what he was going to do that day. Despite all of this, he chose by faith to keep doing the right thing: to honor God no matter how he felt (or did not feel), and to keep encouraging others to do the same. He did this in spite of the fact that his sermons no longer felt inspired. He chose not to let his lack of feeling keep him from living by faith.

Mike had no idea how long he would have to wait before this condition would change. He didn't even know if it would ever change. Yet he decided to continue on in faith, just as he had done before. This experience went on for two years. Then, just as mysteriously as it came, his sense of motivation and direction returned to him.

Looking back, Mike's experience caused him to grow in his faith, realizing he could still do what was right despite how he felt, or didn't feel. He also experienced God's faithfulness despite his condition. In addition, he is now able to encourage others to do the same whenever they go through similar situations.

One of the things that most pleases God is when we live by faith. If you want to make God happy, live by faith.

Seasons of waiting are such opportunities.

It is during your time of waiting that you get to express your faith. It doesn't take faith when everything is going well. It doesn't take faith when you know exactly what is going to happen next, and when it will happen. The Lord lets us see in part. He gives us just enough information for what we need, yet not so much that we are robbed of our opportunity to walk by faith. So, with what He does give us, we walk by faith concerning the unknown. Walking by faith is putting our trust in one thing we do know — that He is faithful and that He will do as He has promised. Despite the unknowns (present circumstances, unanswered questions, etc.), we move forward in faith, believing that He will make it all happen and will make it make sense.

Do not think that you lack faith just because God has not yet answered your prayer. The very fact that you have continued to seek Him demonstrates your faith. While He is preparing the answer, seeking and waiting for Him is an expression of your faith. When the time comes and He answers your prayer, faith for what you requested will no longer be needed, for you will have your reward of your faith.

Walking by faith is like assembling a puzzle, where all the pieces resemble various parts of your life. By themselves, the pieces may not make sense. Initially, you have no idea how they fit together. Many of them may seem not to belong. Just looking at all of them may even seem overwhelming and confusing. But the Lord already knows how it will look once assembled. And if you are willing to trust Him and cooperate in faith, eventually, one piece at a time, it will all come together. If you let Him, He will assemble all the pieces of your life into a beautiful masterpiece (Philippines 1:6)!

Here are some thoughts about faith:
Faith is refusing to let your fear keep you from your destiny.

It is exercising the truth that God is always on time.

It is believing that what God has promised will happen, even though you are not sure how.

It is trusting that God is bigger than your circumstances.

It is realizing that the road may not be easy, but that with God, the destiny is not impossible.

It is knowing that God holds the future, even though you may not know what the future holds.

It is continuing to move forward, even though God has not answered all your questions.

It is trusting that although you don't understand why things are happening, you will understand, once God is done.

It is not just believing that God *can* do certain things, but that He *will* do certain things.

Faith is believing for what you cannot see. The reward is seeing what you have believed.

Faith is not attempting to make sense of your circumstances. Rather, it is trusting that everything will make sense, once God comes through.

It does not take faith to go with the crowd. Faith almost always goes where many will not go.

Faith goes where you have not gone before.

Believing is knowing what God can do. Faith is putting belief into action. It is not faith unless it is applied.

Faith is inviting God to do great things in your life that you cannot do. It does not take faith to do the things you can do.

It is trusting that though you might be where you don't want to be, God will make sure that you get to where you need to be.

It knowing that all obstacles are but road signs that say you are headed in the right direction.

It is remembering that no matter what lies ahead, you can say, "I know that God has already gone before me, and He is already there."

It is knowing that eventually all the pieces will fall together.

It is knowing that, despite lack of proof, God is able, and that is proof enough.

Faith is not knowing how we are going to get there and what will be the end result. It is taking one step at time, trusting the Lord along the way.

Faith is not forcing God to do what you want Him to do. Rather, it is believing what He has told you He will do, especially when you make decisions based upon what He has told you to do. When you do this, you are putting your faith into action.

You don't need a word from God like Abraham received, or a dream like Joseph's, to begin exercising your faith. God has already given you many promises.

In the Bible, God has told you that you are forgiven whenever you confess your sins (I John 1:9). By faith, refuse to stay in guilt or self-punishment. Go on with your day, forgiven. God has told you He will always be with you. He has told you He loves you. Express your faith by refusing to live in shame and rejection.

God has promised to give you wisdom if you ask (James 1:5). Exercise your faith by asking. If He doesn't answer right away, trust that He will give the answer when you need it.

Another way to exercise your faith is by making decisions based upon God's character. God is good. Choose to believe that He is, and that He has good things in store for you, despite your present circumstances. Do so by retaining a positive attitude, responding with a grateful heart, and anticipating good things from Him.

Remember: while waiting on the Lord, exercising faith is essential, not optional!

Application

- What will you be doing today as an expression of faith in God?
- What was the last thing God told you to step out and do in faith?
  - ○ Recall the ways He encouraged and reminded you to do it.
  - ○ Spend time renewing your commitment to do as He asked.
  - ○ Give thanks to Him for what He will do.

Endurance and Perseverance

It is for discipline that you endure;
God deals with you as with sons;
for what son is there whom his father does not discipline?
Hebrews 12:7

And not only this, but we also exult in our tribulations,
knowing that tribulation brings about perseverance;
and perseverance, proven character;
and proven character, hope;
and hope does not disappoint,
because the love of God has been poured out
within our hearts through the Holy Spirit
who was given to us.
Romans 5:3-5

The Big Fish

When I was about twelve years old, my father took me fishing in the Sea of Cortez in Mexico. From our little boat, I hooked up a fish — a really big fish. I was so excited! But I had no idea what I had gotten myself into.

I felt a big jerk on my pole. I got him! The next thing I knew, my fishing line was being stripped from my reel. The fish was running. I started reeling it in. I reeled and reeled and reeled…and reeled. Yet, no matter how fast I tried to reel, the fish seemed to be winning. I watched in frustration as the spool of my line got smaller and smaller. And then…the fish let up. Relief! (So I thought.)

I took advantage of that moment and continued to reel, attempting to retrieve all the line the fish had taken. No sooner had I reeled in what seemed like a mile of line than the fish was off and running again.

My father could see my frustration and that I was getting tired. But instead of taking the pole away from me, he urged, "Whatever you do, do not let go of the pole!"

I was in pain and drained of energy. My arms ached from reeling. My back was becoming sore. My hands were throbbing from the pain of gripping the pole with all my might. The early signs of blisters were forming on my palms. Frustration and aguish were written all over my face. I began to wonder, "How much longer can I keep this up? Will it ever end?" Despite all this, I decided I had better do as my father instructed: "Don't let go of the pole!"

Back and forth the fish and I went. I would reel in the line, and the fish would run. Over time, the fish was becoming more tired. So was I. Yet I kept reeling. It was either me or the fish. It seemed like it would never end, but eventually, I prevailed. I landed the fish — and it was a big one!

At that moment, something amazing happened to me. Despite the exhaustion, I was thrilled! I was elated! Everyone in the boat was cheering! Call me crazy, but I found myself wanting to catch another fish! (What was I thinking?!) The thrill of catching the fish now superseded all the pain and struggle. Sure enough, I baited the hook and threw my line back in again.

"Let's catch another one!"

Because I endured the pain and persevered, I received my reward. Not just the fish, but the joy of overcoming. Looking back, I realized something. If my father had interfered at any time, he would have robbed me of my joy. I would never have learned that I can go beyond what I think I can do — that I can accomplish great things, despite my difficult circumstances and apparent limitations, as well as the pain telling me to quit. Instead of taking over, my father stayed present and guided me through the experience. As painful as it was for me, he allowed me to participate in the process and to have the victory. In the end, character was imparted, and I learned that I do not have to be controlled by my pain.

Discipline

When we are born, we are not naturally equipped with self-discipline. As a matter of fact, we are more inclined to be lazy and undisciplined, seeking ways to do the minimum required, to avoid difficulties and suffering. Therefore, we need someone to assist us in the process of becoming self-disciplined.

16

Years ago, I started to workout — something I had never done before. To help me, I had a coach who set up a workout plan based on my goals, and we met on a regular basis. From the moment we started, I realized just how out of shape I really was! My body ached, complaining the whole time. It was a painful experience. I did not like it. Yet my coach would encourage me and push me beyond what I wanted and what I thought I could do. But after a few weeks, my body stopped complaining. I actually began to look forward to working out, especially as I began to see progress and feel better. Because I hung in there, I began to reap all the benefits that come with working out.

I now workout on my own, challenging myself and making new goals as I improve. I would most likely not have achieved such self-discipline if it wasn't for my workout coach. I now appreciate what my coach did for me — pushing me despite my pain and what I thought were my limitations.

The Lord's discipline is similar. He puts circumstances in our lives to expose areas that need to be worked on. He allows us to experience consequences from the choices we make, so we might learn from them. He places people in our lives who rub us the wrong way, so we might learn to love others. He sends people who challenge us to be the best we can be. I have often found myself saying, "Just when I think God has stretched me as far as I can stretch, He somehow finds more 'stretch' in me to be stretched!"

As with all discipline, in order to benefit us, it is up to us to cooperate with it. If we just endure it to get it over with, we will fail to learn what it is meant to teach us. We will not be fit for what He has in store for us next. So we will either fail when we get there, or in His mercy, He will put it off until we learn what we need to learn. We may have to repeat a season of discipline in some new way until we get it right. So His discipline is for our good, to make us ready for the next thing He has in store for us.

Allowing times of waiting in our lives is one way God disciplines His children. He does not discipline to punish us; He does it for our good. His goal is to bring out the best in us while removing the not-so-best. He creates circumstances that — if we choose to cooperate and not avoid — will bring forth traits we would not have otherwise. He will often put us through times

17

when we must persevere and endure, in order to develop our character. Even though it may be challenging, He is right there with us, encouraging us not to give up. When it is finally over, we discover that we are capable of more than we thought. We realize that all the persevering and enduring was worth it.

Some Thoughts about Perseverance and Endurance

We often use the words, "perseverance" and "endurance," interchangeably. While there are similarities, there are differences.

Endurance is the ability to go the long haul. It is your capacity to weather a challenge or difficulty. Enduring times do not last; only enduring people do.

You know you have passed the test of endurance, not because the difficulty is gone, but because the difficulty no longer controls you.

Perseverance is the determination to continue, and to not give up, no matter what difficulties you face, in order to accomplish something. It is to keep on keeping on. It is more about commitment to a goal than any pain you must face. It is about your dedication to complete a task you set out to do. It is the choice to enter into the arena of difficulty in order to acquire an intended objective.

Whatever you do not persevere through today, you will only have to deal with later. Each day you persevere, you are one day closer to overcoming. If you fail to endure today, tomorrow is a gift — to try again.

Endurance often has to do with putting up with difficulties others create. It's having to tolerate them until things change or let up.

"Love...endures all things" (I Corinthians 13:7).

Perseverance has more to do with yourself — having to press on, despite your weaknesses and shortcomings. Self is the challenge. Trials and testing try your character, revealing what you are made of. They are the process in assisting you in overcoming your limitations. Thus, perseverance is the choice to not give in to your lack.

Perseverance is not *thinking* that you can do something. Rather, it is *proving* you can. It is thinking "I can" in action. And when you're done, it becomes *knowing* you can. Perseverance turns possibilities into experience, theories into realities, and "I *might* do it," into "I *did* do it!"

Whatever you persevere through and overcome, in that arena you gain authority. This allows you to speak into the lives of others, challenging them that they can overcome, too.

When God solves your problems, you have faith in His abilities. When God does not solve your problems, He has faith in your abilities. This is the essence of persevering.

Perseverance is like an athlete's determination to cross the finish line. No matter how many times he falls down, he gets back up. Endurance is that, despite the exhaustion and the pain of falling down, he keeps on going.

Persevering reinforces the fact that, no matter your circumstances, you always have a choice. You may not like your options, but you always have a choice. Yes, you might face situations where you feel like you have no options (or at least, no good ones). But what this really indicates is that you don't *like* your options — so you rule them out as options, and label them as impossibilities. This is because the other options would require perseverance or some sort of personal sacrifice on your behalf. If the truth be known, you are either unwilling to do what is needed, afraid of what it will take, or unsure that you have what it takes. This is where perseverance comes in. If you give it a chance and choose perseverance, it will show you otherwise. Given enough time, perseverance will prove that impossibilities are merely long delays that are eventually overcome.

While perseverance is more about my choice to face a challenge, endurance is more about having to tolerate pain and suffering. Both preference and endurance are necessary in life.

You endure in order to overcome hardship. You persevere in order to overcome a character flaw and build character. Endurance has to do with your capacity, while perseverance has to do with your determination.

Perseverance is the opportunity to move beyond, "this is just the way I am," and move into, "look what I have become!" In reality, "This is just the way I am" is an excuse to not persevere.

Let's say I go on a hike with the intended purpose to reach the peak of a mountain. Along the way it starts to pour down rain. The wind begins to blow. I become wet and cold. In order to get to my desired goal, I will need to endure the hardship of rain, wind, and cold while persevering against temptation to give up and head back the other way. But, once I have reached my destiny, I will gain the deep satisfaction that I have overcome all the obstacles that I encountered. In addition, I get to see the tremendous view from the top of the mountain! I now have the knowing that I can climb other such mountains. And I now know that it was all worth it.

We all have our challenges to face, and most of the time, they are not enjoyable. We may endure a difficult marriage, a wayward child, a hostile neighbor, difficult co-workers, controlling bosses, illnesses, emotional troubles, financial struggles, or family issues, to name a few. During such times, we persevere against impatience or apathy, wanting to retaliate or gossip, being tempted to flee or give into addictions, bad attitudes and behaviors.

Yet, if given enough time, and if we choose to endure and persevere, what may have once seemed impossible is now conquered and doable. For through the faithfulness of the Lord's discipline and our choice to persevere and endure, a transformation has taken place, ending in proven character. Thus, when similar future challenges come our way, we are less intimidated. We can now translate our experience to new challenges that come our way: "Since I endured the conditions and persevered despite my limitations, I know I can face the next one." In addition, we can encourage others, so that they, too, can climb their mountains.

I will let you in on a key insight. To the degree that you cooperate with the Lord's discipline, to that degree it will go much better for you, and the quicker you will learn what you need to learn. Once I have learned what I am to learn and He has instilled in me what He has intended, it is usually soon thereafter that the season of discipline passes.

While you wait, be faithful to endure and persevere, knowing that good things are in store!

Application
- What was a challenging experience in your life that was very difficult, and you weren't sure you could do it?
- What was it like when you overcame, despite how hard it was?
- What are some of the ways the Lord has disciplined you?
- When it was over, what was the result?
- What area in your life is the Lord presently attempting to discipline?
  - Spend some time giving thanks to Him for what He is going to do.
  - List some ways you can cooperate with Him during this time.
  - Ask for His help in doing so.

Those Who Did Not Wait

Rest in the Lord, and wait patiently for Him;
do not fret because of him who prospers in his way,
because of the man who carries out wicked schemes.
Cease from anger and forsake wrath;
do not fret; it leads only to evildoing.
for evildoers will be cut off,
but those who wait for the Lord,
they will inherit the land.
Psalm 37:7-9

The Job

In my early 20's, I got a job as a valet at a restaurant. The extra money was helpful while I was going to college. When Christmas break came, I worked one week for a friend as a painter. While driving his vehicle, I got into a fender-bender. Fortunately, the damage was so minor that both parties decided not to make a claim on their insurance.

When I got back to college after break, I was asked to consider working as a valet at a different restaurant. I thought this would be a better opportunity than my present valet job. The pay was good, and I would be able to work with my friends. The interviewer asked if I had been in any recent accidents. Because I wanted the job so much, I reasoned to myself that the incident was not in an "official" accident, since no claims were filed. So I said "No" — and I got hired.

Looking back, I now realize that God had allowed my fender-bender while graciously sparing me any insurance claims. He had done this so as to guide me in my next job decision. He knew I would be asked if I had been in accidents. If I had told the truth, I most likely would not have been hired. But, I would be where He wanted me to be. And even if they had hired me, I would have had assurance that it wasn't because I manipulated the situation. But instead of telling the truth and waiting to see what the Lord had in store for me, I lied, reasoning away what I had done.

Ironically, a few weeks later I dented a car while working at my new job, and I was fired. I was now without any job. As a result, I missed out on what the Lord had in mind for me. Perhaps I would have gotten a promotion at my previous job. Perhaps He would have had a different job waiting for me if I had not insisted on the one I manipulated my way into. I do not know.

What I do know now is that, more importantly, the Lord was trying to remove my tendency to manipulate situations. He was trying to teach me to trust Him. Although I failed by not being willing to wait, I did learn some valuable lessons. And sure enough, the Lord has since provided me other such opportunities, so that I might get it right.

The Car

I remember a story about a man who decided he would no longer go into debt over purchases. We will call him "Larry." Not too long after making this decision, Larry became in need of a car, and made his need known to the Lord in prayer. As time went on, he grew impatient. It got to the point where, rather than continue to wait, he got a loan and bought a car. He rationalized his purchase because of the great deal and low interest rate.

Unbeknownst to Larry, the Lord had put it on another man's heart to give him a car. When the man went to give the car to him, he saw that Larry already had one. So he never gave him the car.

I don't know if the two men ever talked. But I do know that if Larry had held to his conviction, not only would he have received a blessing, but the other man would have been blessed as well. Besides no monthly payments, Larry would have had an amazing story to share, encouraging others to trust in God for provision.

Yet our Lord is good. He gives second chances. If and when the Lord brought other opportunities to Larry, hopefully he got it right — but only if he chose the next time...to wait.

To Wait or Not to Wait

I looked through the Bible for stories of people who had to wait and chose to do so. I was quite surprised as I found over fifty of them! From these I was able to glean many encouraging insights and applications. For your benefit, many of these stories are explored in the next section of this book. But first, we will take a look at those who chose **not** to wait. We can draw tremendous insights from their stories as well.

It can be argued that whenever we sin, we are not waiting upon the Lord, since we are deciding to not wait and see what He had in store for us if we had not sinned. Obviously, in the Bible there are a lot of examples of people who did this. They were given opportunities to wait upon the Lord over periods of time — to do what was right, and to resist doing what was wrong. Unfortunately, when those periods were over, they had failed to wait upon the Lord.

When I considered those who did not persevere and endure during their time of waiting, I made an interesting observation. I discovered that there are less of them as compared to those who did wait.[1] It made me realize something wonderful about our Heavenly Father. He is invested in our getting it right. He wants us to be successful in our times of waiting. Therefore, He wants to encourage us — to wait and persevere, and to receive the reward of having done so. This is why He gave us so many examples in the Bible of those who did faithfully wait. Most of these were just ordinary people through whom God did extraordinary things. This gives you and me hope.

As I reflected on these stories, I realized something else about God. Each story reveals an aspect of the generosity of His grace. Even though there were consequences for those who did not wait, each was still given an opportunity for grace. While it is true that they missed the previous opportunity, they were given a chance to walk in God's grace for whatever new and different opportunities that followed. The key was this: if they were willing to humble themselves, they would see His grace and the opportunity to walk in it. If not, they would have missed it again.

As you read through the following stories, take time to reflect, for you may draw additional insights and encouragement for your own life. Know that if you have had times of failing to wait, the Lord's grace is still there for you. You can get it right the next time.

The Nation of Israel: On Our Way to the Promised Land!
Remember this day in which you went out from Egypt,
from the house of slavery; for by a powerful hand
the Lord brought you out from this place.
Exodus 13:3

The Preparing-You-for-Your-Destiny Plan
Alias: The Getting-Rid-of-that-Slave-Mentality Plan

Duration: 2 year (plus many days) plan[2]
Scriptures: Exodus 14:1-30; Numbers 14:1-38

The Lord needed to remove the slave mentality out of the Israelites. He had delivered them from their circumstances as slaves in Egypt. Now He needed to deliver them of their ways of thinking. He wanted them to learn that they could trust Him. So, on their way to the Promised Land, He was preparing them. The Lord couldn't afford to take a group of fearful whiners into the Promised Land who would break rank at the first sign of any danger or trial. He was giving them opportunities to grow in faith. Dividing the sea and destroying the army of Pharaoh were just two of many such opportunities.

When things got a little rough, the first thing the Israelites wanted to do was run back to the "comfort" of all that they had known before. (This is a typical response from those who have not yet yielded to the Lord's work in their life.) Longing for "leeks and onions,"[3] they seemed to forget all the oppression they had experienced as slaves. Going back to Egypt was not a real option.

Unfortunately, during their travel time to the Promised Land, the Israelites failed to learn their lessons. The consequence of not choosing to trust the Lord was that the parents' generation would not be allowed to enter the Promised Land.

God's Grace
During their two-year season of preparation, the Lord knew that the Israelites had a lot to learn. That is why He gave them so many opportunities to get it right — ten of them![4] They did not have to get them all right. They just had to eventually get one

thing right, and that was to learn to trust the Lord. Despite the Lord's grace, they made the same mistake over and over again. And it cost them.

Yet, in spite of the consequence of not entering into the Promised Land, the parents were given the opportunity to hopefully teach their children not to make the same mistakes as they had. Their past experiences — even the bad ones — were opportunities to pass wisdom to their children.

In addition, God's grace was extended toward their children. Although they had to put off going into the Promise Land for forty years, they were given the chance to choose to learn what their parents hadn't. Thus, they were given the opportunity to enter the Promised Land.

God's Plan

Know this: that if it feels like you're being put off from your destiny, the Lord is actually preparing you for it. He is working out of you old ways of thinking and living. This season is a gift from Him, an investment in you and your future. Understand that it is normal for it not to seem so at the moment (which usually means you are on the right track). Trust that everything you are going through right now — even if it doesn't make sense — is to make you into your best for what is yet to come.

Yes, change is hard. It means letting go of the familiar. Be willing to let go of the comforts of the past and embrace change. The change you are experiencing means that something better is coming. Know that for each day you live, you are one day closer to your destiny. This season will pass, but it is vital that you pass the test. The Lord is in this.

God has grace for you, but don't take it lightly. For if you do, at some point you will have to live out the consequences of failing to take advantage of the grace He has given you. So do your best to try to get it right the first time.

We all have times when we have failed. God wants to redeem these times by allowing you the opportunity to pass your wisdom on to the next generation. Wisdom is gained through experiences — good and bad. You have learned a lot. So God has given you a powerful testimony to speak into the lives of others. Do so.

Use your time of waiting to learn from whatever you are going through. Glean wisdom from the previous generation. Take to heart the warnings and admonitions they give. Taking these to heart will save you a lot of trouble. Be the generation that gets it right. And know that this season of waiting will pass.

The Nation of Israel: The Golden Calf

If Your presence does not go with us, do not lead us
up from here. …Is it not by Your going with us,
so that we, I and Your people, may be distinguished from
all the other people who are upon the face of the earth?
Exodus 33:16

The Wait-for-Moses Plan
Alias: The What-Matters-More-to-You Plan

Duration: 40 day plan[5]
Scriptures: Exodus 32-33

Moses went up on the mountain and was gone for 40 days. While there, God was giving him instructions. Instead of waiting for Moses to return, the people became impatient and felt they needed to do something. Instead of choosing to resist this urge, they did something impulsive. Under Aaron's direction, they took it upon themselves to make a golden calf.

There were consequences for their actions. But what is fascinating is that God gave the people a chance to repent for being so obstinate.

Furthermore, He gave the Israelites grace for the sake of their leader. Initially, He told them He would longer go with them. Instead, He would send His angel with them when they entered the Promised Land. But Moses said to the Lord that if His presence would not go with them, it would not be worth going. So the Lord said He would go with them.

God's Grace

God's grace during their forty-year wait was the opportunity to rid them of impatience. It was a gift — to build character into them so they could become trust-in-God-driven rather than impulsiveness-driven.

Despite their failure to wait, God's grace was given in the opportunity to choose Him. The offer of the Promised Land and His angel as His representative was a good thing. But there was something better — His presence.

God's Plan

Wait for the Lord's instructions. You do not need to help God. Resist the urge to make something happen when it seems like God is not doing anything. This season is designed to teach you that God is in charge despite what what is not happening. It is a time to teach you patience. It is a time to teach you that you do not have to be controlled by your impatience.

During your time of waiting, resist the urge to do something impulsive. The waiting is an opportunity to put to death your habit of being driven by impatience and the urge that you must do something. Trust that God will come through.

Yes, God wants to bless you; He wants to give you what He has promised. But He also wants to see if you want the Giver more than His gifts. As wonderful as any of His blessings are, how much more wonderful it is to know and want the Lord's presence in your life. This is often the very thing He is trying to teach you during your time of waiting. You can settle for good. But why settle for good when you can have better?

The Nation of Israel: Let's Take It Anyway

...it will not succeed. Do not go up, or you will be struck down before your enemies, for the Lord is not among you.
Numbers 14:41-42

The Wait-for-God's-Timing Plan
Alias: The God's-Timing-is-Best Plan

Duration: 40 year plan[6]
Scriptures: Numbers 14:20-45

Over the course of a two-year period, the Israelites disobeyed and tested the Lord nine times. Despite this, He was willing to give them another chance. The prospect of entering the Promised Land was one of the main reasons they had left Egypt. One would think they would be on their best behavior, as they were about to fulfill this goal. Yet they disobeyed once more, making it their tenth failure.

The Israelites were without excuse. The Lord had given them many opportunities to find reasons to trust Him. They had seen Him perform many signs and wonders. Daily, they had seen the manifestation of His presence in the cloud, and nightly, in the pillar of fire. They had experienced His protection and provision repeatedly. There was no reason for them to not trust Him. So, because of the persistent demonstration of their unwillingness to change, they would have to wait forty years before entering the Promised Land.

Realizing this, the Israelites did not want to wait. Instead, they decided to take the Promised Land in their own strength. Yes, they had admitted that they had sinned, and the Lord had forgiven them. But the Lord was not with them to enter the Promised Land at that time. They presumptuously tried to take the land anyway, and this ended up being a disaster, for it was not time to do so.

God's Grace

God's grace was that despite their unwise and presumptuous decision, He gave the Israelites another chance as a nation to enter the Promised Land. Though they would have to wait forty years, and the parents' generation would not be allowed to enter, the next generation was given the opportunity to do so. The key was to be willing to wait for the Lord's timing.

God's Plan

God wants you to fulfill the destiny He has for you. But if you try to make it happen without Him, it won't go well. If He is not in what you are about to do, then it will all be in your own strength and efforts. You will make yourself vulnerable to the attacks of the enemy. So, avoid making presumptuous decisions.

If you wait for Him, He will make happen what needs to happen. He will do great things, and you will get to come along for the ride!

God's timing is what you are waiting for. It is worth the wait, even if it means being put off for quite a while. God has not put things off in your life without reason. His timing is best. Meanwhile, make yourself ready as you pass through this season of waiting. When the time is right, you will enter into what He has promised, and His presence will be with you.

Saul: Fear the Lord or Fear Man

…You shall wait seven days until I come to you
and show you what you should do.

I Samuel 10:8

The Opportunity-to-Trust-God Plan
Alias: The Fear-of-Man-Removal Plan

Duration: 7 day (or more if need be) plan[7]
Scriptures: I Samuel 10:1-8; 13:8-14

Saul had become Israel's first king. This entailed a lot of responsibility, since so many people looked to him for leadership. One day he was given clear instructions by Samuel. He was to wait seven days for Samuel to return. At that time a sacrifice was to be made, so as to seek the Lord's favor.

This was a God-given opportunity for Saul. God wanted to rid Saul of his fear of man. All Saul had to do was to wait. Saul's enemies were mounting for battle and his own army was scattering, but the Lord wanted Saul to trust Him despite his circumstances. Although it appeared that Samuel was not going to come in time to give a blessing before going to battle, the Lord still wanted Saul to wait. Unfortunately, Saul gave in to his fear. Instead of trusting while he waited, he took it upon himself to offer the sacrifice. When confronted, he gave many excuses about why he felt compelled to not wait. They were as follows:

- "I saw that the people were scattering from me" — Saul trusted in his army, rather than trusting that God would honor his obedience and come through. He may also have been concerned for his reputation. What would people think if he waited any longer, and didn't do something?
- "You did not come within the appointed days" — Saul shifted the blame to Samuel, rather than patiently waiting for him and taking personal responsibility for not waiting.
- "The Philistines were assembling at Michmash" — Saul feared the threats of others instead of trusting in the Lord's timing and protection.

- "I have not asked the favor of the LORD." — Saul had good intentions, but bad timing.
- "So I forced myself and offered the burnt offering." — Saul believed the lie: "I had no choice."

God gave Saul the opportunity to forfeit his struggles and weaknesses in exchange for trusting the Lord. If he had waited and trusted Him, Saul would have been set free from many of his fears. The end result would have made him into a better man.

What was wrong wasn't that Saul had fears; it was that he gave in to them. As a result, he ended up forfeiting his position as king. Every day until the day he died, Saul continued to make decisions based upon his fears.

God's Grace

God's grace toward Saul was that Saul was given the opportunity to someday come to repentance. Saul could have done so anytime during the remaining years of his life. It was a God-given second chance to be free of his fears.

As hard as it would have been, at any time Saul could have humbled himself before the Lord by surrendering his throne to David. In addition, he could have used his temporary position as king to make a smooth transition for David. Imagine the example of repentance Saul would have demonstrated before the people if he had. What a tremendous heritage he would have left!

In addition, Saul had the example of his own son, Jonathan. Jonathan was the next in line for the throne. Despite knowing this, he did not see his friend, David, whom he loved and honored, as a threat, as a threat. Instead, Jonathan chose to walk in the security of God's plan and not base his identity on fear of man, prestige, title, entitlement or power.

Lastly, at any time, Saul could have called upon the Lord to help him in any way he found it difficult to humble himself. And God's grace would have been there for him.

God's Plan

God puts you into situations where you must wait, not so that you can fail, but so you can become a better person. His desire is to remove those things that hinder you from being truly effective and successful. Waiting will bring to the surface your fears and compulsions. Acknowledge them and resist them. Ask for the Lord's help. The more you resist, the less influence they will have over you. The Lord is preparing you for what He has in store for you.

Know that you always have a choice. You may not like the options, and they may be limited, but you always have a choice. Though you may not like your present circumstances nor be able to change them, you can always choose how you will respond in the midst of and despite your circumstances.

While waiting, do not let the choices you can't make keep you from the ones you can. The Lord is teaching you to trust Him despite what you cannot do. Do what you can by choosing how you will respond in the midst of your circumstances.

Trust that the Lord is in control. While waiting, dare to resist your fears, and see how God will come through. Allow the waiting to put your fears to death. This season of waiting is a gift to you from the Lord.

Concerning those times when you may have failed to wait, humble yourself, so that you will not miss the next opportunity to get it right. The Lord can redeem your efforts, despite whatever you may have done.

The Faithful vs. the Unfaithful Servant
Be like men who are waiting for their master when he returns
from the wedding feast...
Luke 12:36

The Be-Found-Ready Plan
Alias: The Be-a-Servant Plan

Duration: as long as one's life plan[8]
Scriptures: Luke 12:35-48

Jesus told a parable about servants who were to be found waiting for their master to return. He used it to illustrate how we are to be as servants of God. While away, the master expected his servants to be just as faithful as if he were present. Several attributes are expected of such servants:

- To be dressed in readiness — prepared and standing by to do what is asked when called upon
- Keeping their lamps lit — ready both day and night, while keeping things maintained
- Watching for their master — expectantly looking out for his coming; not distracted by other things
- Found faithful — doing what the master expects, whether or not he is present

Rightfully, the master was not happy with those who did not heed his instructions. The servants who did heed them were wise for doing so. To such servants, the master will entrust even more.

God's Grace
God's grace is that He has told us ahead of time how we are to be. He has given us instructions that we can fulfill, no matter what place we are in life.

In addition, He has not yet come, allowing us to undergo the discipline of getting ready and becoming watchful.

35

God's Plan

While waiting, God expects you to do your part. During this time, prepare yourself. Learn to be disciplined. Whatever lessons He is trying to teach you, learn them now. It is in your best interest not to avoid the challenges He has placed in your life at this time. No task is insignificant or too menial. Be a good steward with the little things. Eventually, He will entrust you with more, as you are faithful.

Be watchful for the Lord by spending time daily with Him. Develop your sensitivity to His voice and His ways. In this way, you will be made more able to follow when He directs you.

What was the last thing God asked you to do? Do this very thing. Don't put off what He has instructed you to do. Although completing a task is important, being found faithful doing it is even more so. Rather than focus on getting it done, focus on being found faithful doing it. If you do, you will most likely find yourself getting it done.

Be found as a faithful servant during this season of waiting.

The Prodigal Son
Let us eat and celebrate; for this son of mine was dead
and has come to life again; he was lost and has been found.
Luke 15:23-24

The Come-to-Your-Senses Plan
Alias: The Come-to-Life Plan

Duration: as long as it takes plan[9]
Scriptures: Luke 15:11-32

In the story of the prodigal[10] son, the son did not want to wait
for his father's death in order to receive his inheritance. In
Hebrew culture, this was a tremendous insult. It was like saying,
"I wish you were dead!" His father's wealth was more important
to him than their relationship.

Despite the son's immaturity, his father gave him his portion
of the inheritance. He allowed him to make his own decision,
even if it was foolish, and despite the sorrow he must have felt
concerning his son's choices. He knew that, whatever the cost, it
would be worth it if it would cause his son to come to the
understanding that relationship with his father was far more
valuable than anything else. Until the son came to see this for
himself, he was lost and dead. And the son didn't even know it!

The son was lost because he had fled from the very thing that
would bring him the most joy and satisfaction — relationship
with his father. He thought he could find fulfillment elsewhere.
So he became all the more lost.

The son was dead because he thought he could find life in
living lavishly. In the end, this was no life at all. When his
money ran out, so did his friends and his lavish living. He was
left hungry, empty and alone.

One day, the son "came to his senses." He realized that what
he had pursued had not brought him life. While he was at his
lowest, he remembered that his father's hired men had food to
spare. So he returned home, hoping to earn his way back as one
of them. But his father had different plans.

His father ran to meet him, embracing him. He clothed him
and gave him back his place in the family — all at no cost. It was

37

at this point that he truly understood how lost he had been. Upon experiencing his father's unconditional love, he realized he could never earn it but that he was only to receive it. He now was no longer lost as he realized that his place was in relationship with his father.

God's Grace

God expresses His grace as a loving and patient Heavenly Father. He knows that our relationship with Him is more valuable than anything else. He waits for us to eventually come to the same conclusion, as He patiently endures our immaturity. He knows that even if it costs us the loss of things we hold dear, it is well worth the lesson. He is always waiting for us, even when we fail to return to Him.

God's Plan

Often the Lord allows us to go through times of waiting so we will learn that our relationship to Him is more valuable than anything else. Sometimes, when we are unwilling to wait, He lets us have what we think will make us happy, just so we can learn this valuable lesson. He will let such a season run its course until we come to our senses.

Our relationship with our Heavenly Father is not so much about the things He can do for us or give to us. Rather, it is about who He is in relation to us. It is about going on the journey together, seeking Him and spending time with Him.

You can wait or not wait. The choice is yours. If you wait, the Lord will use your waiting to develop your relationship with Him. If you don't wait, you may be one who needs to learn by experience through immature choices. Though it may cost you, the Lord will use this to teach you that He is the source of life and joy. Either way, God wants you to learn this vital lesson, and He is there, waiting for you.

The Disciples: Not Staying Awake
My soul is deeply grieved, to the point of death;
remain here and keep watch with Me.

Matthew 26:38

The See-If-You-Can-Wait Plan
Alias: The Learning-to-Be-Strong-in-Spirit Plan

Duration: 1 hour (3 times) plan[11]
Scriptures: Matthew 26:37-46[12]

Jesus was about to face the most difficult time in His life —
His crucifixion. Taking the disciples with Him, He instructed
them to keep watch with Him as He sought His Heavenly Father
in prayer. While Jesus was praying, the disciples fell asleep. So
He awakened them, saying, "So, you men could not keep watch
with Me for one hour? Keep watching and praying, that you may
not enter into temptation; the spirit is willing, but the flesh is
weak." Then He went back to praying. Ironically, three times
they fell asleep, failing to do as Jesus had requested.

God's Grace
God's amazing grace was that despite the disciples' failure to
keep watch for even one hour, the Lord never held it against
them. Jesus requested their support during a time when He was
"...very distressed and troubled" and His soul was "...deeply
grieved to the point of death." They were given the opportunity,
in some small manner, to give support in return for the many
times Jesus had supported them. Despite their failure to do so,
He did not reject them. Instead, He had great plans for the
disciples — to use them greatly for His kingdom.

Soon after Christ's resurrection, the Lord gave them an
opportunity to get right what they had failed to do, when He
instructed them to wait for the Holy Spirit.[13] And so they did.
After His ascension into heaven, they gathered together and
prayed while they waited. Sure enough, they were present and
ready when the Holy Spirit came. As a result of waiting, amazing
things happened![14]

God's Plan

Though there may have been times when you have failed to do what the Lord had instructed, He is not through with you. He still has plans for you. Do not discredit yourself because of past failures. Move forward so that when the next opportunity comes, you will see it and take hold of it.

Times of waiting are opportunities to grow stronger in spirit, giving less into the weakness of the flesh. The Lord takes you through such times so that you will learn to come against the flesh's resistance to the things of the Spirit.

The Lord's plans will succeed with or without you. But, despite you and your past, He invites you to participate in what He will accomplish. Know that He has invited you. You are important to Him. Whatever He asks you to do, He needs you to do. He needs your support. Just as He has done, He asks of you to consider: "Father, not my will, but Your will be done."

Application

- What are some times when you did not wait?
- What fears and doubts did you give into when you did not wait?
- What was the source of your fears and doubts, and why do you think you had them?
- What does God have to say about your fears and doubts?
- What could you do differently the next time this happens?
- In what ways has and is the Lord giving you His grace?
- What can you do to walk in His grace?

Endnotes

[1] There could be more, but the seven listed in this book stand out the most in the Bible.

[2] Exodus 12:2; Numbers 10:11; plus travel time to the wilderness of Paran (Gen. 12:16) and forty days spying the land (Num. 13:25).

[3] Numbers 11:5

[4] Numbers 14:22

[5] Exodus 24:18

[6] Numbers 14:34

[7] I Samuel 10:1; 13:8

[8] No specific time is mentioned, other than to be ready at all times.

[9] The duration is unknown, but we do know it was as long as it took for the son to come to his senses.

[10] A prodigal is a person who spends money in a recklessly extravagant way (*Oxford Dictionary*).

[11] Matthew 26:40

[12] See also, Mark 14:33-44.

[13] Acts 1:4-5

[14] Acts 2

Waiting upon the Lord

Yet those who wait for the Lord
Will gain new strength;
They will mount up with wings like eagles,
They will run and not get tired,
They will walk and not become weary.
Isaiah 40:31

So, what does it mean to wait upon the Lord? If you have been a Christian for a while, you will know that this is a very important thing to do. Just look at the benefits found in the above verse, and you can see why. There are many other verses that reinforce how important it is to wait upon the Lord. Here are just a few:

Those who hopefully wait for Me will not be put to shame (Isaiah 49:23).

For from days of old they have not heard or perceived by ear, nor has the eye seen a God besides You, Who acts in behalf of the one who waits for Him (Isaiah 64:4).

Wait for the Lord; be strong and let your heart take courage; yes, wait for the Lord (Psalm 27:14).

Do not say, "I will repay evil"; wait for the Lord, and He will save you (Proverbs 20:22).

The LORD is good to those who wait for Him, to the person who seeks Him. It is good that he waits silently for the salvation of the LORD (Lamentations 3:25-26).

But how does one "wait upon the Lord?" What does that look like? How do you do this in your everyday life? If you are like me, you will want to take advantage of the blessings that come when waiting upon the Lord. So it sure helps to know how to do it.

One thing that helps me understand "waiting upon the Lord" is what it means to **not** wait upon the Lord. Knowing this helps me recognize when I might be tempted to not wait.

How to <u>Not</u> Wait upon the Lord

From the previous chapter, we can glean from the mistakes of others, as to what it means to **not** wait upon the Lord. Here are some more examples:

<u>Going Back to Old Ways</u>

Shortly after leaving Egypt, the Israelites began to miss the comforts and foods they had previously enjoyed. It isn't wrong that they missed these things. Rather, it was that they did not choose to believe that their time in the desert was temporary and that God had something even better for them. They allowed wanting to become whining. Wanting to go back to Egypt meant becoming slaves again.

Our old ways consist of bad habits, addictions, sinful behaviors, etc. But they also consist of seemingly good things, such as comforts and enjoyments. The Lord will often challenge us or move us out of our comfort zone, inviting us into change. When this happens, acknowledge that change is uncomfortable; but don't let that keep you from what God has in store for you. Know that going back to old ways means choosing to become a slave to those things again. Trust Him that your time in the desert will pass, and that He has better things coming your way.

<u>Not Trusting the Lord Despite His Promises</u>

The Lord gave the Israelites wonderful promises about their future. He even gave them a prelude to what He could and would do, by all the signs and wonders He performed on their behalf. Yet, with the exception of Moses, Joshua and Caleb, they all lost sight of this. They took their eyes off the Lord, and focused on their circumstances. They let circumstances dictate whether the Lord was trustworthy, instead of submitting their circumstances to Him.

Whatever promises the Lord has given you, know that He will fulfill them, for His promises to you are greater than your circumstances.

Giving in to Impatience

The Israelites allowed impatience to tell them what to do. Sure, it was hard waiting for Moses to return. But that was no reason to do what they did. On top of all this, Aaron gave in to the lie, "Well, I had to do something," and then blamed the people for what he did. As a result, they missed out on what the Lord had in store for them.

Know that whatever urges you may have to manipulate your circumstances, this is the very thing the Lord is trying to free you from. Whatever excuses you are tempted to make about why you feel compelled to have to do something (knowing it truly is not the right thing to do), God is giving you the opportunity to resist. Dare to not give in to impatience, and see what the Lord will do for you!

Being Presumptuous

After realizing they had failed to trust the Lord for the tenth time, and knowing they were not going into the Promised Land, the Israelites decided to enter it anyway. This backfired. Perhaps they did not like the fact that they had had to wait for forty years. Perhaps they were not willing to accept the reality that they had missed their opportunity. Either way, it was not time for them to enter the Promised Land.

When the Lord tells you to wait, then wait. Stay within the timeline and boundaries He has given you. Yes, ask Him if He will possibly change it. But do not presume that you can disrespect His limitations without consequences.

The Lord has a good reason for His timing. It is for your best. If you have missed an opportunity, accept your loss; but be sure not to miss the next one. Presume the best from the Lord, and that His timing is perfect.

Concern for Reputation

Admittedly, it is difficult dealing with what others may think or say about us. One may have to sacrifice reputation in order to do the right thing. King Saul was faced with this choice. Instead of being obedient to the Lord by waiting, he allowed concern for reputation to dictate his decision. It cost him.

The Lord puts us in such situations to free us from this concern. True freedom is found in no longer being concerned about what others think about us, but only about what the Lord thinks. Wait for the Lord to deliver you from what others think. Resist the urge to compromise.

Blaming Others

Shifting blame was a convenient way for King Saul to avoid taking responsibility for his actions. This did not work — nor does it ever work. The Lord's intention was to teach Saul to trust that He was in control despite delays. But Saul failed to wait.

Yes, others may fail to do their part (or it may appear that they have) but this is never an excuse for not waiting. Understand that on God's timetable, what may appear to be a delay is really God creating an opportunity for Himself to be glorified. Just think what would have happened if Saul had chosen to wait despite Samuel not showing up on time!

Fearing Man

Rightfully, King Saul was concerned about the Philistines assembling their army. But instead of submitting his concerns in prayer to the Lord and then waiting and trusting Him, his concerns became fears. He gave in to his fears, and allowed them to compel him to believe he had to do something. He was given a chance to either fear man or fear the Lord.

Try to remember that it is always better to fear the Lord than to fear man. Fearing man is never a good reason to not wait upon the Lord. If you wait upon Him, you will see Him come through in ways you have not imagined.

Excusing under the Guise of Good Intentions

It was indeed important that King Saul should seek the favor of the Lord. However, he was given specific instructions on how and when he was to do this. Instead of waiting, he excused his actions under the guise of good intentions. This only showed that Saul did not believe that God was really in control despite all the problems going on.

Good intentions are never a good reason to decide, "I had to do something!" when you know you are supposed to wait upon the Lord. It is like saying, "Because God is not doing something, I had better do something." Instead, trust that God is up to something, and the only something you need to do is to wait for Him.

Believing the Lie: "I had no choice!"

"What would you have done?" "I had no choice!" These are excuses, not reasons. King Saul did have a choice. He may not have liked the choice to wait, but that was no reason not to do so. His choices were to either give in to his fears or to endure them despite all the obstacles he faced. It was his fears that were telling him he had no other choice. Unfortunately, he gave in to them, and made excuses for his choice.

"Waiting upon the Lord" means choosing not to give in to your fears. Remember, you do have a choice — to give in to your fears or to resist them while you wait. Although it might be hard, make the right choice, and see what the Lord will do.

Choosing to Not Be a Good Servant

In the parable of the good servant, one servant was not faithful during his time of waiting. He did not use his time wisely, so when the time came for him to be called upon, he was not ready.

Sure, you may feel like you are not getting anywhere in life. You may feel unimportant or that what you are doing is insignificant. But don't let this keep you from being faithful right where you are.

Preferring the Gifts over the Giver

In the story of the prodigal son, the younger son learned an important lesson in a painful way, but it was well worth it. He thought life was in what his father could give him materially, when life was right in front of him — a love relationship with his father.

Be thankful for all that God gives you, but always seek the Giver over what He gives. When He seems to not be giving you what you want, choose to wait, realizing He is worth more than anything you could ever want.

Giving in to the Flesh

Our flesh is not very good at waiting. It wants what it wants when it wants it. When we give in to our flesh, we are choosing to not wait upon the Lord. So while waiting on the Lord, learn to resist your flesh and walk by His Spirit.

Taking Revenge

"Do not say, 'I will repay evil.' Wait for the Lord, and He will save you" (Proverbs 20:22). When we decide to do unto others the evil they have done to us, we are definitely not waiting upon the Lord to see how He will save us and deal with the situation.

What are we to do while waiting for the Lord? "Do not repay evil with evil or insult with insult. On the contrary, repay evil with blessing, because to this you were called so that you may inherit a blessing" (I Peter 3:9 NIV).

Manipulating Others or Your Situation

We are to do our best and to be persistent, diligent and wise in all we set our hand to do. In addition, we should do all we can to minimize problems and resolve issues. After we have done all we can, we are not justified in manipulating others or our situation to get things done. Neither are we justified whenever we compromise our convictions. For when we choose to believe that "the ends justify the means," we are no longer waiting upon the Lord.

The Lord does not need our help; He wants our faithfulness. He knows what He is doing. After doing all you can without dishonoring the Lord, trust that your present limitations are God-given, and that He has a good reason for this. Wait for Him. Otherwise, as in the two stories at the beginning of this chapter, you might miss out on a blessing.

Being Irresponsible

To say, "I am waiting on the Lord," but to neglect being obedient and doing what you can right where you are, no matter what your circumstances, is not waiting upon the Lord. It is being irresponsible. For instance, if you need to get a job, you don't just sit idle, waiting for some random person to phone you so they can hire you. Instead, you do all you can by looking for job opportunities, filling out applications and improving your skills. You wait for what you can't do while doing all you can do.

The same is true when waiting upon the Lord. It is never an excuse to neglect your responsibilities: to be obedient, to exercise faith and to do good to others, as well as to do your best. As a matter of fact, waiting upon the Lord involves being all the more diligent in doing these things in the midst of your circumstances.

Seasons of Waiting

When you wait, you are looking to someone or something to tell you what to do, and how and when to respond. You are yielding to the authority of someone or something to show you how you should be or what to do next. It is yielding to their final say, despite what others may be saying. So, to what or whom do you look?

If you think about it, when it comes to **not** waiting, many of your choices come down to allowing yourself to be controlled or directed by your feelings or by others. Being afraid is not the problem; nor is being anxious. Obeying your fear is; allowing your anxiousness to dictate your actions. Feeling pressured by the opinions of others can be challenging — but you still have a choice. Yes, we all struggle with change, the unknown, and peer pressure. Although it is good to consider your feelings, you do not have to obey them. When you give in to them, you are choosing to wait upon them, letting them tell you what to do and how to respond. It is the same when you surrender to peer pressure or the opinions of others.

God purposely and lovingly takes us through difficult situations, so that we might overcome these very things. He does not do this to make us anxious or afraid, but to reveal our dependency upon our feelings, and free us from them. He reveals our anxiousness and fears. His goal is to free us from ways we submit to such feelings. When we choose to wait upon Him, for as long as it takes, the power of these influences will eventually lose control over us. Thus, we gain authority over them.

As you wait upon the Lord, you begin to see that He is not anxious, though you might be. You choose to rely upon His peace, though you might feel fearful. You yield to His rest in the midst of your unpredictable and chaotic circumstances. Waiting upon the Lord is not necessarily a sign of a lack of fear. Rather, it is relying on the Lord's calmness in spite of your fear. It is choosing His authority, His assessment and His response to your situation despite your own evaluation. It is not just knowing He is in control despite your circumstances; it is responding and making decisions that demonstrate that you believe He is in control.

Though many things may influence us, they do not have to control us. Though we wrestle against these things, they do not have to have the final decision. This is often the very reason for waiting upon the Lord — to teach us that though these things at times are very difficult to resist, they do not have to rule us. The Lord has the final say, and we choose to rest in that.

Waiting upon the Lord

The Bible often speaks of the relationship between a servant and his master, to illustrate waiting.[1] A good servant anticipates the needs of his master. He learns how his master thinks and what his preferences are, so he can better serve him. He makes preparations in light of such understanding, making good use of his time while waiting. He puts the needs of his master above his own. He does not allow other things to hinder his availability. Because of this, he is not easily swayed or distracted by other things. If he must choose between what his master's and someone else's request, he chooses his master's, even if what he asks is hard. A good servant does all this willingly. It is his joy to serve his master.

All these things are involved when we wait upon the Lord.

Waiting upon the Lord means looking to Him for the answer and for change. Rather than looking to our circumstances, our feelings, and others to tell us what to do or how to respond, we choose Him. If everything is going crazy and the Lord is at peace, we choose to be at peace. If the storms of life are raging while He is taking a nap in the back of the boat, then we choose to relax, take a nap with Him, or perhaps even do some fishing.[2]

Here are some thoughts about waiting on the Lord:

Waiting means resting in who God is, despite your circumstances.

It is responding according to God's character in the midst of your circumstances.

It is believing He is greater than what is going on around you, and that He is in control.

It is recognizing your need and dependency upon the Lord, so you become emptied of yourself, so that when it is time, He fills you with Himself.

---

[1] Luke 12: 36-48
[2] Luke 8:22-26

It is a time of preparation as the Lord reveals what needs to be removed from your heart (self-focus, unforgiveness, lies, mistrust, etc.) so that you can be ready for what He has next.

It is yielding to His authority regarding who He says you are, and how He sees your circumstances.

Although you might consider all the input and advice given by others, you look for the Lord to have the final say.

While you endure the passing of time, you rest confidently that He will come through as He has promised, even if it appears that He is doing nothing.

It is refraining from being disobedient, though you might be tempted, while being diligent to do good and to be faithful to Him.

It is being willing to take action at the right time, when the Lord directs you, resisting the urge to do otherwise.

It is doing all you can in the midst of your circumstances and despite your limitations.

It is focusing on what you can do, despite what you can't do, knowing that this is all He wants you to do — and that He has a good reason for it.

It is choosing to believe that God has a good reason for what is happening, even if you don't know what that reason is at this time.

It is knowing that the Lord's timing is perfect, and choosing to act accordingly, not doing something impulsive or ahead of His timing.

Isaiah 40:31 speaks of gaining "new strength" when one waits upon the Lord. This is so true. The opposite is also true. When we wait upon worry, this tells us how to respond — to be worried. Thus, we grow weary while worry saps our strength. The same is true with fear, anxiety and so many other such things. They wear us out as they cause us to fret about things we can do little to nothing about; thus, draining us of our energy, time and resources.

As we begin to turn from such things and to the Lord instead, strength comes, as we are no longer being controlled or manipulated by them. When we wait upon the Lord, our energy and resources are no longer being depleted by things that once held our attention. Having our focus on Him brings us into rest — for He does not worry. He does not fear. He does not get anxious. He does not give in to peer pressure. Neither should we.

How to Wait upon the Lord
<u>Live within Your God-Given Limitations and Boundaries</u>
We wait upon the Lord by living within the limitations and boundaries He has instructed us about, or has allowed in our lives. Limitations consist of the restricted amount of resources, energy and time that we have at a given time. He is control. Yes, you may ask Him to remove your limitations. But until He removes them, stay within them.

Some permanent boundaries are those He has made clear in the Bible. For example, we are to tell the truth, and are not to lie. They also may consist of any specific instructions He has given you. For example, He has told you to remain in your circumstances for now.

The Lord has given limitations and boundaries for the very purpose of what He wants to accomplish in you and in your life. When it is time, He may remove or change those limitations and boundaries. While you are where you are, you do all you can to make it better and to make the most of your circumstances. As you do, don't do anything that would dishonor or be in disobedience to Him.

When you choose to go beyond God's limitations and boundaries, you are choosing to not trust Him. Basically, you are saying that God does not know what He is doing, and that you have to do something to help Him out. You are saying that He is not in control.

I have learned over the years that whatever lessons I avoid now, I will only have to learn later. My circumstances change, but the lessons to be learned will be the same.

For instance, at one point it was better to stay where I was, waiting for the Lord, than to be driven by ambition, worry, and the "need" to make more money. I almost took another job to escape the difficulties of the job I already had. Looking back, I am so glad I didn't. It would have cost me more time and money. And I can almost guarantee that the same difficulty (if not worse) would have been waiting for me at the next job. As a result of staying, I have seen the Lord's provision and blessings in many ways. And I am learning the lessons He is teaching me, right where I am, without all the extra stress and striving.

Make the Most of Your Time

While in prison, Joseph made himself useful and gained favor. The prison guards eventually entrusted him with more responsibility. While the disciples waited for the Holy Spirit, they spent time praying. While Moses was in the desert in Midian, he raised sheep. While we wait for the Lord's return, He expects us to be found faithful in whatever we are doing, however insignificant it might seem. Jesus grew in wisdom and stature and in favor with God and man, all the years before He was filled with the Spirit and entered into His three-year ministry on earth.

So make the most of your time right where you are. Never let your limitations be an excuse to not do all you can right where you are.

Embrace Being Uncomfortable

While you wait, you will be uncomfortable. You will be confronted with various weaknesses, bad habits, excuses and sinful responses. It will not be fun. Do not run from it. Embrace it. The Lord will use your time of waiting to draw your dross to the surface, with the desired end to set you free from it. He has great plans for you, and knows it is imperative that you be rid of such hindrances before you enter into those plans. So the best thing you can do while waiting is to embrace the process. When you do, it will go better, and perhaps the Lord will shorten the season.

Remember that You Always Have a Choice

You always have a choice: to wait upon the Lord, or to not wait upon the Lord. As was said in an earlier chapter, you may not like your choices, but you still have a choice.

Application

- What are the things you find yourself "waiting upon" instead of waiting upon the Lord?
- What makes it hard for you to wait upon the Lord? Acknowledge these things, and ask the Lord for His help.
- What is something that God is or has been calling you to wait upon Him for?
- What are some things you are going to do so as to wait upon the Lord concerning this area?

Those Who Waited

The Lord is good to those who wait for Him,
To the person who seeks Him.
Lamentations 3:25

It Was All Worth It

Raised in a Christian home, Betty became a Christian when she was a little girl. When she was older, she met a man, Charles, who eventually proposed to her. With this news, she went to her parents to see what they thought. Both her father and mother told her, "No! That's not a good idea." Charles was not a Christian. Couples who do not share the same beliefs often experience unresolved conflicts and all sorts of problems. Many Christians who have married an unbeliever did so with high hopes, only to live a lonely and miserable marriage. This was her parents' concern. Yet Betty decided, "I can get him saved!" despite that this is only something God could do and there was no guarantee that Charles would get saved. With that, she married Charles anyway.

From that time forward, Betty was committed to praying for Charles to be saved. She felt in her heart that someday it would happen. During all the years of her marriage, Betty always went to church, and Charles never objected. But Charles would never go. She would always invite him, but he would stay at home. So she and their children would go without him. She and her husband couldn't share with each other about faith in Christ.

About 40 years into their marriage, Betty discovered that she had a brain tumor. During that time and through her surgery, she had lots of support from friends and family. Around this time, Charles would sometimes go to church, but he still did not become a Christian. Betty continued to pray for him.

One year later, Betty had to go for a second surgery. During this time, Betty's pastor visited with Charles and asked, "Charles, don't you think it is time for you to give your heart to the Lord?" Charles answered, "Yep, I think so." And he did! The change in Charles was very evident, as he began sharing his faith freely with others. Even their grandchildren noticed the difference. After forty-one years of waiting, the Lord had answered Betty's prayers! And as a bonus, she eventually got to lead Charles's parents to the Lord.

During those forty-one years, Betty learned that even though the struggle became very hard, the Lord's grace and mercy was stronger. God honored her perseverance. She learned to trust and never give up — for it was all worth it! In Betty's own words, "It all came at my expense, with all those years of praying and getting a tumor. If I had to do it all over, I would have had the brain tumor again, just so Charles would be saved! Stay true to your marriage no matter the cost. And do not give-up on God."

Waiting

In this next section is a list of people in the Bible who endured seasons of waiting. All of them had to endure difficult and trying times, from days to many years.

In most instances, these individuals were given no prior warning that they were headed into a difficult season, and most had no idea how long it would last. All they could do was persevere as they waited it out. Some even went through multiple seasons.

There are many reasons why the Lord had these people go through these experiences. Some reasons were unique. But they all had at least two things in common. First, the Lord was bringing about His eternal purposes in and through them for His glory. Second, He knew that one day their experiences would bring encouragement to others like you and me.

At this time, you may have no idea what the purpose is of what you are going through as you wait. But God is faithful, and He is doing something amazing. He has something wonderful in store for you. And someday He will use your story to bless and encourage others.

One more thing, perhaps like Charles you have been putting off becoming a Christian. If so, I would encourage you to pause a moment and become one right now. Just go to the end of the book to learn how.

40-Day Devotional

...his delight is in the law of the Lord,
And in His law he meditates day and night.
He will be like a tree firmly planted by streams of water,
Which yields its fruit in its season
And its leaf does not wither;
And in whatever he does, he prospers.
Psalms 1:2-3

The following stories from the Bible can be used as a forty-day devotional. Whether forty days or forty years, throughout the Bible the number forty almost always involved a time of purposed focus. It was a season when concentrated time was devoted to seeking, preparing and waiting, often just before a transition or change in life.

Entire teachings and even books have been written about each of the following stories. My hope is that you will glean even more insights than the few I have shared about each one.

May the Lord encourage, strengthen and bless you as you do this devotional. And may you finish well your season of waiting!

Noah: Build the Ark

But Noah found favor in the eyes of the Lord.
...Noah was a righteous man, blameless in his time;
Noah walked with God.

The Let's-Build-an-Ark Plan
Alias: The Be-Faithful-No-Matter-How-Long-It-Takes Plan

Duration: 120 years or less plan[1]
Scriptures: Genesis 5:32 - 6:22

No matter how small or large a task might be, don't let anything stop you from doing something the Lord has directed you to do. No matter how long it takes, keep going. Noah didn't let the following stop him:

- The immensity of the task — the ark was longer than 1.5 football fields![2]
- The unknown — not knowing where he would end up.
- Lack of experience — having no prior experience building an ark or how to take care of wild animals.
- Lack of knowledge — not knowing how all the other tasks would get done. It wasn't Noah's job to gather the animals. His was only to build an ark. He just did his part, trusting that when it was time, the rest would come together.
- Fear of man — wondering what the neighbors would think.

While Noah was assigned no small task by the Lord, he did not let this deter him from starting. He just kept at it, and eventually the job got done. He "...walked with God," doing his part as God had instructed, while trusting God to accomplish what He said He would do.

The Lord would have us focus on being faithful, and not worrying about how everything will get done. Take it one day at time. Complete what you can do today. Don't let anything deter you!

If the Lord has something for you to do, then He will make sure it can be done. Just do a little here and a little there, and eventually it will be accomplished. He has given you all the time you need.

Noah: Live in the Ark
Noah did according to all that
the Lord had commanded him. Genesis 7:5

Day 2

The Let's-Live-in-an-Ark Plan
Alias: The While-You-Wait-How-Will-You-Pass-Your-Time Plan

Duration: 370 day plan[3]
Scriptures: Genesis 7:1- 8:22

Imagine forty days and forty nights of flooding, with the sound of unceasing rain pounding on the roof. Add to this that all the while you are tossed to and fro on the open sea for many days.

Once the rain had ceased, there were still 330 additional days in an ark with all those animals. It must have gotten very smelly after a while! I imagine that Noah was never bored, as there were lots and lots of animals to tend to.

By the way, Noah was never told how long he was going to be on the ark. He had to wait and find out.

Have you ever gone through one of those difficult seasons that it seemed would never end? Perhaps you are in one now. Your conditions are no longer ideal. Your life has become mundane and routine. You have limited choices of what to do and where to go. You may not even like what you are doing. You trusted God and got onboard with His plans, and now you are wondering when whatever you are going through will ever come to an end. There's no going back. There is only waiting.

So what do you do while you wait? For one, you do whatever was the last thing the Lord told you to do. Be faithful right where you are. Continue to go about your life, trusting the Lord while swabbing the decks, cleaning the stalls and maintaining your ship.

It's guaranteed; no matter the duration of your waiting, time will eventually pass. The key is how you will pass your time while you wait. So pass the time well. Your season will eventually come to an end.

And remember, just as the Lord had a rainbow at the end of the journey for Noah, He has something special waiting for you!

Job: Suffering

The Lord gave and the Lord has taken away.
Blessed be the name of the Lord.
Job 1:21

The Trust-God-Despite-My-Suffering Plan
Alias: The I-Will-Bless-the-Lord-Anyway Plan

Duration: several months plan[4]
Scriptures: Job 1:1-22

Job went through a season where he lost everything, short of his own life! He lost his children, possessions, reputation, health and everything he had ever gained. He even lost the support of his wife, who urged him to "...curse God and die." As you read further into the book of Job, you will find that even his friends turned from comforters into accusers, questioning his very character, due to his circumstances.

At one time or another, we have all have had to deal with loss or being misunderstood. So we can all relate to some degree with what Job went through.

Perhaps your circumstances have caused people to question your character: "You must have done something wrong for this to happen." And what about living with unanswered questions: "Why me?" "What do I do now?" Or, you have had to deal with self-doubts: "Maybe I did something wrong." Or doubts about God's care for you: "Where is God?" Maybe, despite having been faithful to the Lord, things you held dear were taken away from you.

So, what was the key to Job making it through his awful experience? He was honest with God, and chose to trust and bless Him, no matter what. He never let go of the fact that all things come from God. More importantly, Job held onto a true understanding of God's character. He didn't let his circumstances dictate to him who God is.

God is good — all the time! For now, trust Him as He rids you of being circumstance-driven. Given enough time, as you persevere, the Lord will lift you above your circumstances.

Abraham and Sarah: The Promise

The Lord did for Sarah as He had promised. **Day 4**
So Sarah conceived and bore a son to Abraham in his old age,
at the appointed time of which God had spoken to him.
Genesis 21:1-2

The Trust-God-to-Fulfill-His-Promise Plan
Alias: The God-is-Faithful-Despite-Us Plan

Duration: 25 year plan[5]
Scriptures: Genesis 12: 1-7; 15:2-5; 17:15-22; 21:5

Abraham's original name was Abram. Sarah, his wife, had been known as Sarai. Abram was 75 years old[6] when the Lord first promised him that he would have a son. Up until that time, Sarah had been unable to bear children.

The name, Abram, means "exalted father."[7] Imagine living 75 years with a name like that, and yet having no children to show for it. Then one day God tells you that you will have a son, and you have no idea that you will have to wait an additional 25 years until this is fulfilled! It makes you wonder how many times Abram and Sarah felt discouraged.

We see that discouragement in Abram at the age of 86. He and his wife decided to "help" fulfill God's promise. They were getting old and thought that they had better do something. They got their eyes off of Him who is able to do anything, and onto their circumstances. Thus, Ishmael was born. Yet, despite their foolishness, God was faithful, and one day, Isaac was born.

Ishmael represents man's efforts. Isaac represents faith: that what God has promised, He will fulfill as we trust Him to do so.

The Lord doesn't need us to "make" His promises happen. He only wants us to have faith in Him and grow in that faith! For when you wait, letting God fulfill His word, then you will have the privilege to truly say, "He did it!"

God will fulfill His promises concerning you! He will do this despite the "Ishmaels" you have birthed in your life. He is faithful. He doesn't need your help to get things done. He is using time to grow you in your faith and to see if you will trust Him. When it is the right time, He will do just as He has said.

59

Abraham: The Man of Faith
And Abraham believed God,
and it was reckoned to him as righteousness,
and he was called the friend of God.
James 2:23[8]

The Making-of-a-Man-of-Faith Plan
Alias: The God-Is-for-You Plan

Duration: 25 year plan
Scriptures: Genesis 22: 1-14

Initially, Abraham was not a man of faith. While he was waiting for the Lord to fulfill His promise of a son, the Lord made him into a man of faith.

At the first opportunity to act by faith, Abraham failed. Shortly after Abraham moved to the Egypt, he became afraid that one of the Egyptians would kill him and take Sarah as his wife. So, out of fear for his own life, he instructed Sarah to tell others that she was his sister.[9] In light of God's promise to him, he had no reason to do this. God had said to Abraham that he would have a son. Since, at that time, he didn't yet have one, how could anyone take his life?! Even after God had rescued him despite his folly, Abraham did this very same thing again in a different place.[10]

Another time, Abraham faltered in his faith when he and Sarah agreed to fulfill God's promise of a son via their own means. Despite this, the Lord did not give up on him.

Then, one day, Abraham got it right. When asked by the Lord to sacrifice his son, he demonstrated his faith through obedience. God spared his son and blessed Abraham, promising to bless others through him. He also changed his name from Abram to Abraham, which means, "father of multitude."[11]

Our Lord is in the business of changing you. Trust Him. The Lord will make you ready for your destiny. Your job is only to cooperate. What He is taking you through now is necessary for your future. No matter how many times you have failed to trust Him, get back up again. Don't be discouraged. He is gracious, and He is committed to you getting it right. Don't give up. He has good things in store for you. And He wants to bless others through you.

Sarah: The Woman of Faith

And by faith even Sarah,
who was past childbearing age,
was enabled to bear children because she considered Him faithful
who had made the promise.
Hebrews 11:11

The Making-of-a-Woman-of-Faith Plan
Alias: The God-Will-Make-It-Happen Plan

Duration: 25 year plan
Scriptures: Genesis 12:2-3; 17:15-21

Sarai was 65 when the Lord first gave the promise of a son.[12] While waiting for this to be fulfilled, there were two times when her husband, Abraham, did not honor and protect her. He did not stand in faith, but gave in to his fear by not publicly acknowledge her as his wife. Instead, he assigned her the duty of protecting him! In addition, thirteen years later, she still didn't have a son. Discouraged, she told Abraham to consider an alternative plan, and he gave in to her. What she really needed was for him to be strong, to stand in faith on behalf of both of them during her time of faltering.

Sarai was not without her moments of doubt. She laughed when reminded that she was to have a son in her old age. But in the end, Sarah became a woman of faith.

Prior to age ninety, Sarah's name was Sarai,[13] which means "nobility."[14] The Lord changed her name to Sarah, which means "princess."[15] It was as if the Lord was saying, "I know all that you have gone through, feeling not honored. But you are more than just nobility. You are also a princess — precious to Me!"

The Lord is for you. Though you have struggled with doubts and discouragement, He is not ashamed of you. He knows the disappointments you have faced and the people who have let you down. He will remove your shame.

God is able to fulfill His promises concerning you. He is able to do so despite your present condition, your circumstances, your age (young or old) or your perceived or real limitations. This is what He is working into your heart, so that you will walk in this for yourself and impart it into others.

61

Jacob: Waiting to Get Married

So Jacob served seven years for Rachel,
and they seemed to him but a few days
because of his love for her.
Genesis 29:20

The Looking-Forward-to-Getting-Married Plan
Alias: The How-Will-You-Respond-When-Tricked Plan

Duration: 7 years[16] plus an extended 7 years plan[17]
Scriptures: Genesis 29:15-30

Jacob was looking forward to getting married. To have Rachel as his wife, seven years of labor were well worth it. His love for her made the time pass quickly.

Unfortunately, when it came time to have Rachel as his wife, he was tricked by Laban into marrying Leah instead. Yet Jacob did something amazing. He chose not to become bitter! Nor did he let such treatment ruin his love for Rachel. He also chose to be honorable, being willing to work another seven years for Rachel.

Having something to look forward to, this helps pass a time of suffering. It enables you to look beyond your hardships and focus on the prize. When you allow yourself to be distracted by present difficulties, you begin to lose sight of what is to come.

Consider Jesus: "For the joy set before him he endured the cross, scorning its shame, and sat down at the right hand of the throne of God."[18] This verse doesn't say that Jesus felt joyful while suffering; rather, that we are His joy. He had the joy of knowing that what He was to go through on the cross would set us free!

Focus past your suffering and on to what is coming once the waiting is over. Do not lose sight of that. Though you might lose sight of it from time to time, do what it takes to get your focus back. Though is always easier to become bitter, choose to do the hard thing. Don't let bitterness ruin any future anticipated joy.

Your present struggles are not without reason. They have a purpose. Someday, they will come to an end. See every day as an investment in the joy that is waiting for you. And remember: you are the Lord's joy!

Jacob: Trying to Make a Start in Life
Jacob said of his father-in-law, Laban:
"[He] cheated me and changed my wages ten times;
however, God did not allow him to hurt me."
Genesis 31:7

The Keep-Working-Hard-Despite-Being-Tricked Plan
Alias: The Learning-to-Deal-with-the-In-Laws Plan

Duration: 6 year plan[19]
Scriptures: Genesis 30:25-43; 31:1-16

Being tricked was not the only wrong Jacob suffered from Laban. Laban also cheated him ten times during his six years of service to him. Talk about in-law issues!

Yet, once again, Jacob did something amazing. For starters, he chose to do his best, serving with all his strength. Jacob endured seven more years of service, in spite of Laban's trickery. Though he may have had good cause to leave his present situation, he chose not to. He did what he knew was right in the midst of difficulties and despite his mistreatment. Once the Lord had instructed him to leave, it was then he left.

It is really hard when you have trusted someone and they don't keep their promises. You keep your end of the bargain, and they choose to not keep theirs. What do you do?

For one, make the most of your time while in this season of hardship. This is a time preparing you for your future. You have been given an opportunity to be your best, despite all the obstacles and troubles. Don't let them get the best of you. Be your best. A day will come when you will rise above your circumstances. The proof will not be that your circumstances have changed, but how you have changed in spite of them. This is what the Lord is working into you.

Do not let someone else's lack of character become an excuse not to do your best. Rise above it. Be better than them. Don't get even; trust in the Lord. Follow His instructions. Learn all that you are to learn during this season. He will inform you when it is time to move on to the next thing He has in store for you.

Jacob: Wrestling with God

Jacob said, "I have seen God face to face,
yet my life has been preserved."
Genesis 32:30

The All Night Plan
Alias: The Wrestle-with-God Plan

Duration: 8+ hours plan[20]
Scriptures: Genesis 32:24-30

Jacob had a past, and he was about to face it. He feared for his life because of how he had treated his brother, Esau. Now, just before he was to face his brother, the Lord challenged him to a wrestling match. Jacob could have said, "Not right now. I am really busy at the moment. This is a bad time." On the other hand, perhaps Jacob had no choice. We do know that he wrestled all night and that he didn't call a truce. He gave it his best despite his immediate situation. And then to add to the difficulty, at one point the Lord dislocated Jacob's hip, which seems a bit unfair. But he still didn't quit!

The point of the wrestling wasn't that Jacob might win, but whether he would be willing to wrestle and not quit. Despite the Lord making the wrestling so difficult for Jacob, Jacob didn't give up, not without getting a blessing first. In the end, God not only blessed Jacob for his perseverance and determination, he also changed his name to "Israel," (meaning, "fights with God"). [21]

You will have times of wrestling with God. You will engage Him through prayer. It may be in the midst of an inconvenient time. Don't let that stop you. When you wrestle with Him, do not give up. Go as long as it takes. No matter what He throws at you, take it and keep going. He will do this to see if you will rise to the occasion, no matter the conditions of the match. It is not about you winning the match, but what He is bringing forth in you while you wrestle. There is a blessing waiting for you.

You might have a "limp" after wrestling with God, but it is worth it. Your limp will provide opportunity to speak into the lives of others. Just like Jacob, whenever someone asks you, "How did you get that limp?" you can say, "Let me tell you about the time I wrestled with God..."

Joseph: His Dream

As for you, you meant evil against me,
but God meant it for good,
in order to bring about this present result.
Genesis 50:20

The Fulfillment-of-a-Dream Plan

Alias: The Death-to-a-Vision and Its-Restoration Plan

Duration: 13 year plan[22]
Scriptures: Genesis 37:1-36; 39:1-45:28; Acts 7:9-10

Everything seemed to be going really well for Joseph. Life was good. He had some amazing dreams from God, indicating that God had a special purpose for him. He was favored by his father. Then, one day, it all went bad. Out of jealousy, he was betrayed by his brothers — sold into slavery, falsely accused, stuck in a prison, and twice forgotten. He missed some of the best years of his life. None of this looked anything like the dream God had given him.

Joseph suffered because of the jealousy and choices of others. His brothers chose to take offense at his dreams instead of believing that God's goodness was being expressed for them concerning their future. Their reaction cost Joseph dearly.

Despite all this, every time things got bad, Joseph chose to make the best of the situation. And one day, when it was time, God fulfilled the dreams. Through all this, God was preparing Joseph for a greater purpose. In the midst of it, he could not see it. "Yet God was with him, and rescued him from all his afflictions, and granted him favor and wisdom."[23]

Perhaps you have had a dream or vision concerning your future, yet fulfillment is nowhere to be found. As a matter of fact, everything seems to have gone wrong — quite the opposite of what has been promised.

Know that God will fulfill the dream He has given you. Meanwhile, He is preparing you. Be faithful, and do your best right where you are. Do not take offense at others. Make the most of your time in the place where you are, no matter how difficult it is. The Lord has not forgotten you. The time will come when you will be able to say, "The Lord meant all this for good!"[24]

Joseph: Imparting to the Next Generation
By faith Joseph, when he was dying,
made mention of the exodus of the sons of Israel, and gave orders
concerning his bones. Hebrews 11:22

The It-Takes-My-Entire-Life Plan
Alias: The Leaving-a-Legacy-of-Faith Plan

Duration: 110 year plan[25]
Scriptures: Genesis 50:22-26; Exodus 13:19

Joseph believed in God's promises, made to his great grandfather, Abraham. He believed that someday the descendants of Israel would live in the Promised Land. He believed, even though he never got to see it fulfilled in his lifetime. As a demonstration of his faith, just before he died, he instructed his descendants to bury his bones in the Promised Land. Sure enough, 480 years later,[26] Joseph's bones were finally buried there.[27]

Joseph had faith beyond the years of his own life! He left a legacy of faith for the next generations.

One of our purposes in life is to pass on to the next generation the promises God has made. It is our task and privilege to inform and encourage the next generation regarding what He has in store for them. We are to share of the Lord's faithfulness in our lives. This provides a catalyst of faith, motivating them to believe God for their own lives. We are to reassure them that He has a plan for them, and to impart the vision of what He has given to us. It is our privilege to do this.

This is why God has allowed you to go through what you have. All the seasons of waiting are leaving a legacy for the next generation. What you have gone through and your faith will impact them, even in ways you may not see fulfilled in your lifetime. Your time of waiting in faith is not and will not be wasted.

"...which we have heard and known, and our fathers have told us. We will not conceal them from their children, but will tell to the generation to come the praises of the Lord, and His strength and His wondrous works that He has done" (Psalm 78:3-4).

Jabez: Painful Past

Jabez was more honorable than his brothers.
...Now Jabez called on the God of Israel...
I Chronicles 4:10

The Free-Me-from-My-Pain Plan
Alias: The As-Long-As-It-Takes Plan

Duration: ??? year plan
Scriptures: I Chronicles 4:9-10

Jabez had a painful past, and it followed him for many years of his life. His name means, "pain." He was named after the pain his mother endured when he was born.

Imagine being named "Jabez." Every time you introduce yourself, it automatically begs the question: "So how did you get your name?" And now you have to tell your story. Every time your name is called, you're reminded of what your mother went through. It makes one wonder if Jabez felt that he wasn't a joy, or that he was to blame for his mother's pain. Perhaps he was teased by peers.

One thing is for sure. Despite his past and how he may have been hurt, Jabez decided to seek the Lord for help. We have no idea how long he had to ask God. Days? Months? Years? We do know that he kept asking until he finally got what he was asking for. In Jabez' case, God didn't change his name. Think about it. From then on, whenever someone asked, "How did you get that name?" Jabez could reply, "Well, let me tell you what God did in my life!..." God turned his past, his pain, and his name into a testimony!

Right now the Lord is working a story into your life. He is using, and will use, all the painful things in your life for His glory. He is making you into a living testimony of His faithfulness. No matter what others have said, no matter your past, no matter your pain, ask Him for what it is that you want. No matter how long it takes, seek the Lord. No matter how many times you have given up, get back up and pursue Him.

When it is time, your story will be written. And you too will be able to say, "Well, let me tell you what God did in my life!..."

67

The Nation of Israel: Slaves in Egypt
And the sons of Israel sighed
because of the bondage, and they cried out...for help. ...
God heard their groaning...
and God took notice of them.
Exodus 2:23-25

The What-Does-it-Take-before-You-Finally-Ask-for-Help Plan
Alias: The Help-Motivate-You Plan

Duration: 430 or so year plan[28]
Scriptures: Exodus 1:6-14; 2:23-25

The king of Egypt had a destiny in mind for the Israelites: to be slaves forever, and to fulfill all his personal goals. As long as they stayed in Egypt, they would never enter their true destiny.[29]

Isn't that how it often is?! Rather than leave the familiarity of where we are, we would rather stay, even when things get bad. We know how things work. It's predictable, even though we may not like it. We adjust, rationalize, and make excuses. And, rather than leaving the familiar, trusting God, and heading into the unknown, we would rather stay right where we are.

The Israelites had a destiny: the Promised Land. Yet, it was as if they had forgotten who they were, and that Egypt was only a temporary stay. But one day, they had had enough. They began to cry out to God, and God heard them. The Lord had been waiting all that time for them to finally ask for His help.

Often, the Lord allows our conditions to get worse, so that we will finally be motivated to want change and to do whatever it takes to enter our destiny. He is waiting for us to be willing to let go of the familiar and ask Him for help. Sometimes it's not the place where you are that needs to change. Rather, a change needs to take place in you. He is using your present conditions to do just that.

The Lord is making you uncomfortable. Do not settle for where you are. You were meant for more. Trust the Lord, and do not fear the change that is to come, for in it is your destiny, and the Lord has good things in store for you. No longer put off crying out to the Lord. Don't wait for things to get really bad before you do. And especially, don't wait 430 years before you begin!

The Nation of Israel: The Next Generation

Your sons shall be shepherds for forty years
in the wilderness, and they will suffer for your unfaithfulness,
until your corpses lie in the wilderness.
Numbers 14:33

The Let's-Do-It-Right-this-Time Plan
Alias: The Wilderness Experience Plan

Duration: 40 year plan[30]
Scriptures: Numbers 14:20-35

The prior two years had been preparation for what was to happen next — entering the Promised Land. Along the way, the Lord gave the Israelites many opportunities to learn to trust Him. But instead of taking stock of all the things the Lord had done, the majority continued to complain and rebel. Ten times they did this. Instead of acknowledging what the Lord could do for them despite their fears, they wanted to go back to Egypt.

As a result, they were not allowed to enter the Promised Land. Even when they tried in their own efforts, they failed. By then it was too late. The blessing to enter the Promised Land had passed to the next generation. Unfortunately, they had to wait forty years.

Sometimes we have inherited struggles because of what our ancestors have done or failed to do. This isn't God's punishment. Rather, it is the Lord's way to ensure that our generation does not make the same mistakes as the previous one. He uses such times to prepare us, and to write on our hearts tenacity and determination not to fail to enter our destiny.

Do not see this time as a time of punishment. The Lord isn't punishing you; He is preparing you. He is writing wisdom into your heart so that you won't settle for less. Learn from the mistakes of the previous generation. Make sure to follow through where they did not.

Embrace this season. Learn what you are to learn from it. In so doing you will avoid having to spend an additional season in the wilderness. The Lord is with you, even in the wilderness.

Day 15

The Nation of Israel:
Taking the Promised Land

Be strong and courageous, for you shall give this people possession of the land which I swore to their fathers to give them. Joshua 1:6

The Taking-Hold-of-Your-Destiny Plan
Alias: The Possess-the-Promise Plan

Duration: 5+ years plan[31]
Scriptures: Joshua 1:1-18

When the Israelites entered into the Promised Land, it wasn't without effort on their part. Yes, it was theirs to possess, but it did not come without its challenges. To "possess the land" does not mean just kicking back and doing nothing. It means dispossessing what was there and taking ownership. This takes effort.

Before entering into the Promised Land, four times the Israelites were charged with the command: "Be strong and courageous."[32] Why? Because this was what was required in order to enter into their destiny. Though there were challenges ahead, the Lord said that He would be with them. So all the more, they needed to be strong and courageous.

Never let the challenges you face distract you from knowing what the Lord is capable of doing. When the Lord is with you, you have reason to be strong and courageous. He exhorts you to do so.

Whatever the Lord gives you, He expects you to be a good steward of it. He expects you to rise to the occasion, taking on whatever challenges you may face. He wouldn't have brought you this far to have you give up and turn back. What He has entrusted to you, He knows you have what it takes to be faithful with it.

As with any new thing, there are often challenges where changes and some renovations need to be done. There are strongholds that need to be overcome and removed, left by those who were there before you. As you meet these challenges, you make a place for others to live and thrive. That is why the Lord has put you where you are — so you can make a difference for others. And whatever you do, complete the work the Lord has for you. With His help, you can do it!

The Nation of Israel:
Scattered and Brought Back as a Nation

Then the Lord your God will restore your fortunes
and have compassion on you, and gather you again
from all the nations where he scattered you.
Deuteronomy 30:3

This is what the Sovereign Lord says: I will take the Israelites
out of the nations where they have gone. I will gather them
from all around and bring them back into their own land.
I will make them one nation in the land.
Ezekiel 37:21

The Knowing-God-Is-in-Charge Plan
Alias: The God-Will-Do-As-He-Says Plan

Duration: 1,878 year plan [33]
Scriptures: Deuteronomy 30:1-14

Since the beginning of time, God has had a plan concerning every nation. He brought them into creation, and knows of their destiny. He is presently orchestrating their future for His glory. They all serve a purpose in His plans throughout history.

The Lord kept His promise to Israel. Because of their sinfulness, He scattered them among the nations. He did this, knowing that one day He would gather them back again. Nearly 1,900 years later (May 14, 1948), He made them into a nation again, gathering them from among the nations. This all happened despite the enemy's attempts to wipe out the Jewish people.

This speaks volumes about Who is really in charge of history. No matter how man or the enemy may try to interfere, the Lord will bring about His purposes and plans. No matter how impossible something may seem, the Lord can make it happen.

All promises He has made concerning you, He will fulfill. He will do so no matter what you have done. He will do so no matter what man or the enemy may do, no matter how impossible it may seem, no matter how history may change, and no matter how long it may take. His promises concerning you — consider them already done. He never forgot Israel, and He has never forgotten you!

So be patient. Wait. He will do it!

Day 17   **Moses: The Growing-Up Years**
This is the Moses who said to the sons of Israel,
"God will raise up for you a prophet like me from your brethren."
Acts 7:37

The Trust-God-to-Fulfill-Your-Purpose Plan
Alias: The Not-Take-Matters-into-Your-Own-Hands Plan

Duration: 40 year plan[34]
Scriptures: Acts 7:17-29

As Moses grew up, it was as if he knew his life had some sort of greater purpose. There was something he was to do; some purpose he was to fulfill.

One day, Moses took matters into his own hands in dealing with how an Egyptian was mistreating an Israelite. He killed the Egyptian. It was as if he knew he was meant to help deliver the children of Israel. He "...supposed that his brethren understood that God was granting them deliverance through him" (Acts 7:25). Sadly, it backfired. Moses ran away from Egypt for fear of his life, spending the next forty years in the desert (Exodus 2:15).

Have you ever thought you were destined for some greater purpose? That there must be more to life than what you had done so far? Chances are, you were right. Like Moses, you might not have known how this purpose would be fulfilled. You may have even tried on your own to fulfill it. Most likely, it will still be fulfilled in a way you have never imagined.

You may think you have missed your opportunity. Or, because of your failures, you may feel are no longer qualified. Perhaps you, too, have a past, and you have tried to move on and make a new start somewhere else.

God has been preparing you through all that you have been going through. He will use every event and experience in your life. He will even use your mistakes. Commit these to Him. Someday it will all make sense. Someday it will all come together. For now, try to avoid taking matters into your own hands. Don't concern yourself about making your destiny happen. Be willing to submit all to Him.

For now, just do your best. Trust Him. His timing is perfect.

72

Moses: The Desert Years

Moses: The Desert Years

Moses fled from the presence of Pharaoh
and settled in the land of Midian. Exodus 2:15

[Moses] led the flock to the west side of the wilderness
and came to Horeb, the mountain of God. Exodus 3:1

The Being-Humbled Plan
Alias: The Not-Take-Matters-into-Your-Own-Hands Plan

Duration: 40 year plan[35]
Scripture: Exodus 2:1-15

Before the Israelites ever began crying out, the Lord was already preparing the answer! As a matter of fact, eighty years before they ever asked for help, He had prepared the administrator of His deliverance plan: Moses! Moses spent forty years growing up in Egypt and forty years in the desert as a shepherd. The Lord used these times to prepare Moses as a leader.

During Moses' first forty years, he did things in his own strength and on his own initiative. At the end of this time he became aware that in his own strength he couldn't bring about deliverance.

After murdering the Egyptian, Moses spent his next forty years in the desert being humbled. During those years, all he knew was that he would be a shepherd for the rest of his life. This prepared him as a humble vessel, so that the Lord could use him mightily.

What you have gone through is not without cause. Perhaps you too feel you have failed in your past, and now you are stuck going nowhere. Your day-to-day life may seem mundane and meaningless. As you go through your desert-time, do not despair. Though you may feel useless to the Lord and go through long periods without hearing from Him, know that He is still with you.

The Lord takes us through times in the desert to remove all human effort and ambition, so that our identity and security is no longer in our abilities, knowledge, experiences and strength. Rather, it is in Him. Then, the Lord has a vessel He can and will use mightily. Embrace this time of being humbled.

Know that what you are going through now has a purpose, and that the Lord is preparing you. Know that others have been praying, and that you are perhaps an answer that is in the making and on its way. In time, this will be revealed.

Day 19   **Moses: The Entering into Destiny Years**

By faith Moses, when he had grown up,
refused to be called the son of Pharaoh's daughter, choosing rather
to endure ill-treatment with the people of God than to enjoy the
passing pleasures of sin, considering the reproach of Christ greater
riches than the treasures of Egypt; for he was looking to the reward.
By faith he left Egypt, not fearing the wrath of the king;
for he endured, as seeing Him who is unseen.
Hebrews 11: 24-27

The Entering-into-One's-Destiny Plan
Alias: The It-Is-Time Plan

Duration: 2-year (plus many days) plan[36]
Scriptures: Exodus 3:1-10

When the time was right, the Lord called Moses into his destiny — to administrate the Lord's deliverance plan for Israel, to lead them out of Egypt, and into the Promised Land. All the years prior, the Lord had taken Moses through a process of refinement. Through this, Moses learned the lessons and benefits of endurance. He came to know that there was only one thing worth living for that would satisfy one's soul. And that was the Lord.

The Lord often takes us through different seasons so that we experience the temporariness of what this world has to offer, and that we might eventually know the riches of Him and His ways. You know this is happening whenever you are being challenged to compromise your convictions.

As with Moses, there might be times in life when you will need to make hard choices — choices that may cost you your previous comforts, benefits, and even reputation. You may have to face great obstacles while not backing down, and, as a result, live with the disapproval and reactions of others. But know this: the Lord is working a great work within you. It may cost you now, but it will be worth it.

When you have completed your seasons and the Lord has brought about His work in you, He will bring you into your destiny. You may not see a burning bush, but you will know. Even if, like Moses, you have to wait eighty years, it is not only worth it; the Lord is making you ready!

74

Moses: The Extended Years

Now the man, Moses, was very humble,
more than any man who was on the face of the earth.
Numbers 12:3

Thus the LORD used to speak to Moses face to face,
just as a man speaks to his friend.
Exodus 33:11

The Wandering-in-the-Desert Plan

Alias: The Having-to-Suffer-Because-of-the-Faults-of-Others Plan

Duration: 40 year plan[37]
Scriptures: Deuteronomy 33:1-43

Despite seeing the Lord provide and do amazing things time and time again, the Israelites failed to trust Him. When they were about to go into the Promised Land, they chose to whine and be filled with fear, desiring to go back to their life in Egypt. Therefore, the Lord would not let them enter the Promised Land. For forty years they wandered in the desert until their disobedient generation had died off.

Because of this, Moses had to spend forty years of his life wandering in the desert. This was amazing, to have to live with and suffer the consequences of what others had done, when he had done no wrong. No wonder Moses was called the humblest man who lived!

If the Lord allows you to enter into a "Promised Land" season (a time of blessing and abundance), receive it. It is His gift to you. But, as wonderful as all that is, it will never compare to the riches of eternal things. Moses came to know this. Despite the unfaithfulness of others, he remained faithful, trusting the Lord. Moses even blessed the Israelites before he died. As hard as it may have been, he had learned what really mattered. As a result, he became a mighty servant-leader for the Lord, because his greatest treasure was the Lord Himself!

What you are going through is meant to bring you to a place where nothing else matters but the Lord. Knowing and walking with Him is the greatest reward. He is preparing you, so that He can use you mightily, unhindered by others and your circumstances. He has great things in store.

Joshua: Be Strong and Courageous
As for me and my house, we will serve the Lord.
Joshua 24:15

But I followed the Lord my God fully.
Numbers 14:8

The Serve-the-Lord-Even-When-You-Have-Been-Faithful-and-Others-Have-Not Plan
Alias: The Serving-and-Trusting-The-Lord Plan

Duration: 40 year (plus: 5+ years[38]) plan
Scriptures: Exodus 14:1-9

When the twelve returned who had spied out the Promised Land, Joshua was one of two individuals who stood apart. He saw the same challenges as everyone else, but he brought back a good report. He trusted the Lord. He knew the Lord would help them overcome every obstacle.

Unfortunately, because of those who brought back a bad report and because the people didn't repent of giving in to their fears, the whole community had to wander in the desert for forty years, until the disobedient had passed away. Joshua was not allowed to go, even though he had been faithful and obedient.

Sometimes you through difficult seasons because of the choices others have made. You might be facing obstacles that would not have been there if someone had done their job. These setbacks are now affecting you, costing you time and energy that they would not have otherwise. Perhaps you feel that your opportunity for a "Promised Land" season has been missed.

If this is so, know that God is not punishing you. Instead, He will use this time to shape and develop your character. He knows your heart. He has seen your faithfulness. During this time, choose to forgive those who have failed to do their part and have caused you to suffer. Ask the Lord to redeem your days in the desert. Draw close to him. Like Joshua, take courage. Serve and trust the Lord while you wait. The day is coming when you will enter into your "Promised Land" season.

Caleb: Following Fully

But My servant Caleb, because he has had a different spirit and has followed Me fully, I will bring into the land which he entered, and his descendants shall take possession of it.
Numbers 14:24

The Trust-in-the-Lord-While-You-Wait-to-Enter-into-Your-Inheritance Plan
Alias: The Be-Willing-to-Trust-and-Obey-Despite-Suffering Plan

Duration: 40-year (plus additional fighting time) plan
Scriptures: Exodus 13:26-30

There are several things that distinguish Caleb. He allowed the difficulties he experienced after leaving Egypt to teach him about God's faithfulness. Thus, he came to know that he could trust the Lord, despite the anticipated challenges ahead in the Promised Land. He was committed to going forward and not backward. He knew that if the Lord could see the Israelites this far, then He would surely help them overcome anything. He was also willing to challenge others to get on board, even if it meant taking a stand against the opposing view.

But there was another thing that distinguished him. Like Joshua, he was willing to trust and obey the Lord, even when he suffered because of the wrongs of others. He was willing to serve God and wait for his inheritance. After forty years, he entered the Promised Land and received his destiny.

During your difficult season, take full advantage of this time, and choose to follow the Lord fully. Allow this time to teach you of God's faithfulness. Remember the times when He has been faithful, and know that He will be today, as well as in your future. Desire Him and what He has for you. This will keep you from desiring to go back, and will keep you moving forward.

Don't let setbacks created by others discourage you. Know that even in the midst of this, God has a plan. Be faithful. Serve the Lord. Do your best. Choose to forgive those who have wronged you. Use this time to become a clean and prepared vessel for the Lord.

He has good things in store for you.

Hannah: Praying for Her Desire

[Hannah] gave birth to a son;
and she named him Samuel, saying,
"Because I have asked him of the Lord."   I Samuel 1:20

The Year-after-Year Plan
Alias: The God-Will-Use-Your-Misery-and
Will-Birth-Something-Wonderful Plan

Duration: many year plan[39]
Scripture: I Samuel 1:1-28

As hard it may have seemed, "...the Lord had closed her womb," preventing Hannah from having children. He did this even though she longed to have a child and had never done anything to deserve childlessness. Peninnah, who had children, harassed Hannah about her condition, which often brought Hannah to tears. This miserable experience went on "year after year," despite Hannah's prayers and longing. Yet, Hannah didn't give up. She continued to seek the Lord. And one day she conceived and eventually had a son, Samuel, who became one of the Lord's great prophets. This brought great joy to Hannah (I Samuel 2)!

Whatever misery the Lord has allowed in your life, it is not without purpose. Though it continues year after year, seek the Lord. Allow it to drive you to pray. Even though the harassments of others discourage you, don't give up. Let this be confirmation that you are headed in the right direction. Why else would the enemy try so hard to discourage you? He may not know exactly what is coming, but he sees your faith and determination, and thus, he knows that God is up to something amazing. Know that the Lord births great things through much suffering and prayer.

Don't be satisfied until you have what you are praying for. This is a time to sow much prayer. Though this season may be long, it will be well worth it. Though you have times of misery, know that in the economy of God, this is precious and necessary. He will bring about great things that would not have happened otherwise.

The Lord is about to birth something wonderful through your suffering. Your prayers are being heard. Your suffering is not in vain.

David: To Become King
The Lord has sought out a man after
his own heart and appointed him.
I Samuel 13:14[40]

The Making-of-a-King Plan
Alias: The Necessity-of-Time-in-the-Wilderness Plan

Duration: Part I: 20 year plan;[41] Part II: 7 year plan[42]
Scriptures: I Samuel 13: 1-16; II Samuel 5:4

Even though David was anointed at a very young age to be king of Israel, the fulfillment did not begin until he was thirty years old. It took another seven years until it was completed, with Judah coming under his kingship. During his years of waiting to become king, David was in the wilderness fleeing for his life, dealing with his enemies' false accusations and trying to survive day to day.

Yet despite his circumstances, David wrote psalms to encourage himself, while giving thanks and praise to the Lord. In the midst of his troubles, he sought the Lord and poured out his heart in prayer. Though he had the opportunity to take his position as king, and had been wrongly treated, he chose instead to honor Saul and to trust the Lord. The Lord used this long season to prepare David for his destiny as a man after God's own heart.

During your time in the wilderness, hold on to the promises the Lord has given you. Recall them to mind. Give thanks to Him that He will fulfill all that pertains to you. Allow this time to teach you to trust in Him and not in your own strength. Take advantage of this unique time, and choose to praise Him despite your circumstances. Thank Him for what he has done and for what He will do.

Learn to forgive those who wrong you. Honor others despite how they dishonor you. Lead by example. The Lord is fashioning you for your intended destiny.

When your time in the wilderness has fulfilled its purpose, you will know you are ready. At that time the Lord will fulfill His promises concerning you. For now, make the most of this time by putting your trust in the Lord.

David: To Seek the Lord
Then David said to Nathan,
"I have sinned against the Lord."
II Samuel 12:13

The Inquire-of-the-Lord Plan
Alias: The Humble-Yourself-Then-Move-On Plan

Duration: 7 day plan[43]
Scripture: II Samuel 12:1-22

When David committed adultery with Bathsheba, he tried to cover his sin. He misused his authority, and had Uriah set up to be killed so he could have Bathsheba as his wife. Thus, he added sin on top of sin. He thought his sin was hidden. Yet God knew. When David was confronted with his sin, he immediately owned it. And God forgave him!

But there were still consequences. One was that the child Bathsheba had conceived became sick and was going to die. So David humbled himself and sought the Lord, waiting in hope that He would spare the child's life. The child died anyway, seven days later.

Instead of getting all upset or coming under condemnation or lamenting endlessly, David got up and went on with his life. He chose to walk in God's forgiveness towards him. And although the Lord did not heal the child, David decided to commit himself to the Lord, accepting the consequence of his sin.

We have all committed sins which we regret. Often, there have been consequences. If you have sinned, humble yourself and own your sin. Spend time seeking the Lord. Perhaps He will spare you of some of the consequences. But even if He doesn't, know that He does forgive you. Choose to walk in forgiveness. Do not let regret keep you from walking in God's grace and mercy. Accept the consequences and learn from them.

The Lord has new things in store for you. Do not allow your past to keep you from them. Choose to not let the past rob you of the good things the Lord has for you today.

Day 26

Now I, Nebuchadnezzar, praise, exalt and
honor the King of heaven, for all His works are true
and His ways just, and He is able to humble
those who walk in pride.
Daniel 4:37

The Humbling-of-a-Man Plan
Alias: The Being-Blessed-through-Being-Humbled Plan

Duration: 7 year plan[44]
Scriptures: Daniel 4:4-37

When needed, the Lord will take you through the process of being humbled. He is doing you a favor. It is a gift. What you go through may not seem so, but in the end it will be a blessing.

When humbling you, the Lord will remove from your life things in which you have put your confidence and trust, that are other than Him. These can be such things as strength, accomplishments, talents, intellect, appearance or job. If the Lord has removed or altered what you once put your confidence in, you are most likely in a season of being humbled. Take this as a good thing, and that better things are coming.

Being humbled is one of the best things that can happen to you. It puts everything into perspective. Being humbled allows you to become who you really are in light of who God really is. It frees you from being preoccupied with yourself to being preoccupied with God and all that He is. It allows you to recognize that everything you have, have done, are, and will be, is all because of Him.

During whatever season of waiting you may be in, there is a high probability that the Lord is humbling you. Almost all such seasons involve some measure of this. This is for your best. Embrace it. Do your best to not resist it. This will minimize the need to repeat the process. And perhaps the Lord will shorten your season.

Know that what is waiting for you is praise that will flow freely from your heart for all that the Lord is doing, has done, and will do. And whatever he restores to you will no longer be a hindrance.

Daniel: Praying for Israel

[Daniel] continued kneeling on his knees
three times a day, praying and giving thanks before his God,
as he had been doing previously.
Daniel 6:10

The As-Long-as-It-Takes Plan
Alias: The Continue-to-Seek-God Plan

Duration: 70 year plan[45]
Scriptures: Daniel 9:1-23

Daniel knew why his nation was in captivity in Babylon — because of their sins and iniquities. He also understood the importance of seeking God and offering prayers of confession.[46] He committed himself to pray three times a day, confessing the sins of the people and the iniquities of his ancestors, kings and priests. He did this despite opposition. He did this even if he would never live to see the day when Israel was freed from captivity. He continued in prayer for years!

Despite the King's edict, Daniel continued to pray. As a result, he was persecuted and thrown into the lion's den. The enemy knew the power not of only Daniel prayers, but what he was praying for — God's forgiveness and deliverance. Despite the enemy's attempts, Daniel was delivered, restored, and honored. It was as if God was saying, "Just as I did for you, so I will do for Israel because of your prayers!"

You may have prayers you haven't seen answered for years. Don't be discouraged. Know that God has heard your prayers. Sowing in much prayer is preparing the way, even though you may not see it and nothing seems to change.

When you are discouraged or even persecuted for your commitment to living rightly and honoring God, realize you are on the right path. The enemy wouldn't waste time coming against you unless he felt threatened, knowing that your prayers are being heard by God and that God is about to do something. No matter how long it takes, keep praying.

As you keep to your commitment to prayer, remember the times when God has answered your prayers. Use these for encouragement and to strengthen your resolve. Write down and recall the times when God has given you promises and affirmation.

You are on the right track. You were called for this purpose of this season of prayer. God is going to do something amazing!

Daniel: Praying for an Answer

Do not be afraid, Daniel, for from the first day that you set your heart on understanding this and on humbling yourself before your God, your words were heard, and I have come in response to your words.

Daniel 10:12

The Pray-until-You-Get-an-Answer Plan
Alias: The Persistence-Pays-Off Plan

Duration: 21 day plan[47]
Scriptures: Daniel 10:1-21

For 21 days, Daniel prayed and fasted, seeking the Lord for an answer concerning a vision that troubled him. He had exhausted his attempts to make sense of it. Yet instead of giving up, he continued to seek the Lord for an answer.

Though Hebrews 11:6 had not yet been written, Daniel demonstrated his understanding of the concept it conveyed: "And without faith it is impossible to please Him, for whoever would draw near to God must believe that He exists and that He rewards those who seek Him." Daniel sought God, and the Lord rewarded him with the answer he requested.

God has heard your prayers, even at this time when it seems that He hasn't. The answer is on its way, even though you have not yet received it. The Lord may not deliver it via an angel, but He will answer you. So continue to persevere in prayer. Do not give up just because you cannot figure things out. As you pray and wait for the Lord to answer, allow this time of waiting to humble you.

Though you have no idea of the effect of your prayers, God is moving on your behalf and doing amazing things. Though you cannot see, great things are taking place in the heavens. Your prayers are effective in spiritual warfare. They are very important and significant.

Know that as you persevere in prayer, your faith is what God sees, and this is what pleases Him. Your responsibility is to pray. It is His to make things happen. This temporary postponement of the answer may seem frustrating, but it is really an opportunity for you to exercise, and grow in, your faith. So take advantage of this time of waiting. When the time is right, you will have your answer.

Jesus: The Son of Man
And Jesus kept increasing in wisdom and stature,
and in favor with God and men.
Luke 2:52

The Wait-for-It, Wait-for-It... Plan
Alias: The Continue-in-Preparation Plan

Duration: 30 years (before He began His ministry) plan[48]
Scriptures: Luke 2: 1-52

When God sent His Son into this world, He did not immediately start His ministry. It was thirty years before His ministry on earth began, and all of this was in preparation for His final purpose — His death and resurrection. He came as an infant. He went through all the experiences one goes through as a human — having parents, growing up, and much more. As a child He, "...continued in subjection" to His parents (Luke 2:51).

While he waited for his purpose, Jesus was active. He learned a trade, becoming a carpenter like his father. He increased in wisdom from what He learned and experienced. He increased in stature, and kept His body fit and strong. He also gained the favor of God and man. There were times he would even teach. While he waited, Jesus prepared Himself in these ways.

During your wait, use the time well. Be active. Learn a skill or two; develop your abilities. Be the best you can be at your job. Be in submission to those in authority. Use this time to complete tasks you need to get done. Increase your wisdom, which is the ability to apply knowledge, understanding and experience to making sound decisions. Grow in stature by developing godly character. Take care of your body, keeping it fit. All these things are preparation for what is to come. In this way when the time comes, you will need to be ready.

Your time of waiting is for you to make yourself ready. Then, when you are called to action, you can respond without hindrance. Rest in the fact that you are in a time of God's preparation. Everything you do now is just as significant as fulfilling your later purpose. Like Jesus, be right where you are, making the most of it and knowing that God the Father is in control.

Jesus: The Son of God
When He began His ministry, Jesus Himself
was about thirty years of age. Luke 3:23

But when the fullness of the time came,
God sent forth His Son, born of a woman, born under the Law,
so that He might redeem those who were under the Law,
that we might receive the adoption as sons.
Galatians 4:4-5

The Time-of-Ministry Plan
Alias: The Let's-Do-It Plan

Duration: 3 year plan[49]
Scriptures: Luke 3:21-23

God's timing is always perfect. His whole plan is perfect — even the amount of time He allots to it.

Think about what God did. He sent His Son, who spent His first thirty years not doing any ministry. And then, when He did enter into His time of ministry, it was only for three years, and in an obscure little country, Israel. During His life on earth, He remained in a very small region. And in the end, the nation He came to bless ended up rejecting Him and wanting Him crucified. Despite all this, He did more to affect the entire world — past, present and future — than anyone in all of history!

Like Jesus, don't concern yourself with how the things you are doing for the Father fit into the bigger picture. Trust Him that somehow, they do. Don't think that what you are doing is insignificant. Don't allow yourself to be swayed by the belief that you will be more effective by going beyond the bounds assigned to you. As you continue to trust and follow your heavenly Father, you will always be exactly where you need to be. He will instruct you otherwise, if needed.

As in Jesus' life, the Father does profound things in your life in obscure ways. These may seem obscure to man, but they are by no means obscure to our Father. He delights in confounding the so-called wisdom of man. And often, that is the very thing He is doing and is going to do through our lives. What better way to say, "This was all God's doing," then to use the very circumstances of your life to demonstrate His glory. Know that with God, a lot can get done in a very short amount of time. At the right time, He will direct you.

Jesus: The Savior of All Mankind
…that Christ died for our sins according
to the Scriptures, and that He was buried, and that He was raised on
the third day according to the Scriptures.
I Corinthians 15:4

The Dying-with-a-Purpose Plan
Alias: The What-Only-God-Can-Do Plan

Duration: 3-day plan[50]
Scriptures: Luke 23:33-24:12

Just prior to His crucifixion, Jesus was betrayed by one of His disciples, denied by another, and abandoned by the rest. The people to whom He had ministered turned on Him and wanted Him dead. He went through the most excruciating and horrible experiences, including crucifixion. Lastly, Jesus died. And then God did what is impossible for man — He raised Him from the dead!

All that Jesus went through was worth it. "For the joy set before Him, He endured the cross, despising the shame, and has sat down at the right hand of the throne of God" (Hebrews 12:2). Jesus arose from the dead, victorious over death! As a result, all of us believe have eternal life and the hope of resurrection.

God may be asking you to do something really hard. It may even seem impossible. Even Jesus asked if there could be an alternative plan. Yet He chose to trust His heavenly Father.

Know that our God majors in impossibilities. He does not ask us to do something He is unable to complete. He may not be asking you die on a cross like Jesus. None the less, He is asking you to take up whatever cross you have been given (your challenge) and follow Him.

God will keep His promise concerning you, no matter how impossible it may seem. He will come through. What He brings to death, He can raise to new life. Know that there is joy waiting for you, even though, during your season of dying to self, you may have none.

When it is time, he will restore you and bring you back to life. For now, trust Him.

Simeon: Promise Fulfilled

And there was a man in Jerusalem whose name
was Simeon; and this man was righteous and devout,
looking for the consolation of Israel.
Luke 2:25

The Most-of-My-Life Plan
Alias: The It-Was-Well-Worth-the-Wait Plan

Duration: many year plan[51]
Scripture: Luke 2:25-35

Simeon was waiting for the Messiah. The Holy Spirit had told him he would not die until he had seen the Lord's Christ. Then one day, he saw Jesus as a baby with His parents, and he knew He was the one, as indicated by the Holy Spirit. How long between the promise and his eventual meeting with baby Jesus, we are not told. But we do know that Simeon willingly and eagerly waited for the fulfillment of God's promise, no matter how long it would take. And he was not disappointed.

It makes one wonder, how many others weren't waiting and looking for the Messiah? Had they given up? Or, were some looking but didn't expect a child, and therefore missed it?

Simeon held to the promise God had given him, even to the end of his years. He may have had ideas of what the fulfillment would be like when the day would come. Perhaps he had thought Jesus would be a grown man. Yet, he trusted the Holy Spirit to direct him.

During your time of waiting for the Lord to fulfill His promises, devote yourself to Him. Use this time to develop intimacy with Him. That is what this time is for. Learn to hear His voice and to follow the Holy Spirit. As you do, He will give you greater clarity.

When the Lord fulfills His promise(s), you will recognize it because of your closeness to Him. You will not miss what others miss, for what the Lord is about to do is greater than you have imagined. And when it happens, it will bring you much joy.

The Determined Woman
Jesus said to her,
"Daughter, your faith has made you well; go in peace."
Luke 8:48

The Will-You-Do-Whatever-It-Takes? Plan
Alias: The I-Will-Do-Whatever-It-Takes Plan

Duration: 12 year plan
Scripture: Luke 8:43-48

For twelve years this woman suffered from what appears to have been a hemorrhage. She tried all means available in an attempt to find a cure. Despite all her effort, she was not successful. She even spent all her savings. Yet, she was not willing to give up.

Her social life was nonexistent. She had to live in isolation because she was considered unclean, due to her condition. It makes one wonder if she had to struggle with what others thought of her. Yet, she was not willing to give up.

Then Jesus came to her town...

She decided that despite all her failed attempts and the social humiliation she had endured, she would pursue Jesus. She was willing to go out in public despite her issue. She was willing to risk touching Jesus, despite that she was considered unclean. She was willing to try, even if it meant one more failed attempt.

As a result, she got healed! She was publically restored, and her faith was publically affirmed. And Jesus blessed her with peace.

Do not give up! No matter how many failed attempts. No matter how many obstacles. No matter what it costs you: time, money, effort, etc. Do not give up! Pursue Jesus.

When you touch Jesus, He ends up touching you — and something changes inside. It is completely worth it, no matter what it costs.

Your time of waiting is meant to rid you of being ruled by failure. It is to remove the control of being concerned about what others think. It is to remove from you things that would otherwise hinder you. It is to free you to risk — for a blessing is waiting for you.

The Blind Man

[Jesus] saw a man blind from birth
[and said], this happened so that the work of God
might be displayed.
John 9:1-3

The God-Has-a-Special-Purpose-for-My-Life Plan
Alias: The God-Can-Use-Me-Despite-My-Affliction Plan

Duration: many year plan[52]
Scripture: John 9:1-41

A certain man was born blind. He had to fend for himself, and would sit and beg for subsistence.

One day he encountered Jesus. Jesus applied mud to his eyes, and instructed him to go and wash them. In order to do so, he had to find his way to the pool while still blind. He did it, and came home seeing!

His healing became his testimony: "One thing I do know; I was blind, but now I see!" It was simple, but powerful. The change that took place in his life turned his whole city upside-down! People were amazed. It confounded the religious community. It gave opportunity to reveal Jesus as the Christ. It also blessed the man and glorified God.

Your life isn't without purpose. God planned a purpose for your life even before you were born. No matter what is in your past or the reason why things are the way they are, nothing can thwart God's purposes. Despite your afflictions and infirmities, God can use you and them for His glory.

Seek the Lord, asking him to use your life for His glory. When he directs you, do as He has instructed. Trust Him, even when He asks you to do something despite your apparent weaknesses and inabilities. Though the blind man could not see, he could walk. Use the abilities you do have. Don't excuse yourself from following the Lord's instructions because of what you lack.

Whatever change He brings about in you through your affliction, He will use it to affect and bless everyone around you.

Raising Lazarus from the Dead
This sickness is not to end in death, but for the
glory of God, so that the Son of God may be glorified by it.
John 11:4

The Wait-and-See-What-God-Will-Do Plan
Alias: The Die-to-My-Expectations Plan

Duration: 4 day plan[53]
Scripture: John 11:1-44

Jesus got word that his friend, Lazarus, was sick unto death. He knew that the Father had a special purpose in store despite this situation. So, instead of being moved by the worries of others, He stayed where He was and trusted His Heavenly Father. "For whatever the Father does, these things the Son also does in like manner" (John 5:19).

Eventually, Jesus did leave. But by the time He finally arrived at Lazarus' home, Lazarus had been dead for four days and his body was in a tomb.

Martha's (Lazarus' sister's) expectation was that if Jesus had come sooner, Lazarus would have been healed. But now Lazarus was dead, so it was too late — at least from her perspective.

Sometimes the Lord needs to bring us to a place where we die to our expectations of what we think He should have done, and die to our thoughts like, "If I were God, I would have..." Know that He not only can do what He has done before (like heal people), but He can and will do even greater things.

Don't let your limited experience with the Lord limit what you think He can and will do. This is what faith is for — to learn to believe, and thus, see the glory of God!

During this time of waiting, as hard as it may be, allow yourself to die to your expectations of what God should have done. Instead, believe for even greater things; otherwise He would have done something different. Allow this gift of time to teach you to tune in to what the Father is doing. Know that the Lord can do even greater things. And know that what He has in store is going to bring even greater glory than if He had done what you think He should have done.

Creation Is Waiting

Ever since the fall of man, all of creation has been waiting to be set free from corruption while it suffers.
Romans 8:18-22

The Waiting-for-the-Sons-of-God Plan
Alias: The Waiting-Since-the-Fall-of-Man Plan

Duration: since the fall of man plan
Scripture: Romans 8: 18-25

Creation itself is in waiting. It is waiting for our son-ship in God to be revealed — our adoption as sons, the redemption of our bodies. Until then, all of creation suffers. Ever since sin entered into the world, creation has been subjected to futility. It struggles to operate in its intended design, at its peak performance, while it experiences frustration and decay. But, one day we will see it released and then flourish as God intended. This is why it waits eagerly for the day when God will bring us into glorious freedom as the children of God. Not only will we experience freedom, but so will all of creation!

Do not allow yourself to become discouraged by the decay, futility and oppression you experience and see all around you. Know that someday God will not only set you free, but also all of creation. He is the Creator. At any given moment, He could restore all things. Instead, He has chosen you and me to be a part of this amazing future event — the restoration of creation! For now, we struggle in our unredeemed bodies. Although our present bodies are subject to decay, we know that God will someday give us redeemed bodies.

No matter what your struggles and weaknesses are in this life, better things are coming. No matter what infirmities and afflictions you experience in this present life, know that this is not the end.

Don't let yourself become discouraged by what you suffer. Instead, focus on what is to come. In the meantime, know that God will help you in your weakness. And when the time comes, God will restore and redeem all things!

The Prodigal Son and His Father
But when he came to his senses...
Luke 15:17

But while he was still a long way off,
his father saw him and felt compassion for him
and ran and embraced him and kissed him.
Luke 15:20

The Until-You-Come-to-Your-Senses Plan
Alias: The I'll-Wait-As-Long-As-It-Takes Plan

Duration: as long as it takes plan
Scripture: Luke 15:11-32

Here we have a story about a father and son who both went through a difficult season in their lives. The father went through a season of waiting, as long as it took, until his prodigal[54] son returned from going astray. It was also about a son who was on a journey to maturity, even though he may not have realized.

The key moment was when the son came to his senses. If the father had rescued his son at any time before that crucial moment, his son would have never learned, and would most likely have repeated the same mistake. The father had to resist the temptation to rescue him. Instead, he waited and watched for his son, storing up his love and allowing time to have its way with his son.

If you have a prodigal son, daughter or friend, love them by praying and waiting for them. Anticipate your celebration when they return, but resist rescuing them. Pray that they come to their senses, which is the best thing that could happen for them. You have been given a gift by God — a season of waiting and praying for them. As you go through this season, you will get to share in knowing what the love of our heavenly Father is like. And the joy will be yours when they come to their senses and return.

If you have been a prodigal son or daughter, realize that no matter what you have gone through, God is at work in your life. Know that despite your past, He loves you and wants to restore you. Know that you can return to Him, and that He will welcome you with open arms. Out of His love for you, He knew you needed to learn for yourself so that you would come to your senses. He is waiting for you.

Paul: Getting Turned Around

But when God, who had set me apart
even from my mother's womb and called me through His grace,
was pleased to reveal His Son in me so that I might
preach Him among the Gentiles...
Galatians 1:16

The Being-Prepared-to-Serve Plan
Alias: The Transition Plan

Duration: 3 or more years plan[55]
Scripture: Gal 1:11-23

When Paul[56] became a Christian, his whole life was turned around.[57] Before, he was persecuting Christians. Upon encountering Jesus, he became His servant, eager to do His will — especially after having come to understand all the harm he had done.

Yet, before he began serving the Lord, Paul waited three years. He spent time in prayer and repentance, seeking God so as to unlearn his misunderstandings of God's Word, and to glean from it the truth about Jesus as Messiah.

As a result, Paul became an effective minister for God's purposes. Throughout his life, he was not swayed by men, but was moved by God and his love for Jesus.

Whether it is becoming a new Christian or God bringing you into a season of change, often you need to go through a time of transition. Whether you are a student, friend, employee, leader, or parent, God puts you through times of transition to prepare you before you enter into what He has next for you.

Embrace your season of transition. Learn all you can during this time. It is for your good, so you will be ready and effective for what is to come. Though you might feel put-off, God is preparing you. He is ridding you of things that would otherwise hinder, removing misunderstandings and fortifying you with His wisdom. Learn from Him. Learn to hear His voice in times of quietness so that you will recognize His voice in times of noisiness. And in due time, God will release you into what He has for you to do.

Paul: Delayed Destiny

[Jesus said], "Take courage; for as you have
solemnly witnessed to My cause at Jerusalem,
so you must witness at Rome also."
Acts 23:11

The Delayed-Destiny Plan
Alias: The I-Thought-I-Was-Supposed-to-Be-There-by-Now Plan

Duration: 5 year plan[58]
Scripture: Acts 27:27-28:18

By his own appeal,[59] Paul was supposed to go to Rome. He even had a word from God that he would,[60] yet it took five years to get there, due to delays. On his way, he was put into prison, and later, he was shipwrecked. But instead of getting upset, he trusted that God was in control. He saw that God had given him an opportunity to bless and minister to others. If he had been so focused on having to get to his destiny, he would have missed the journey. For it was Paul who wrote, "And we know that God causes all things to work together for good to those who love God, to those who are called according to His purpose" (Romans 8:28).

Life is often about having to deal with delays. Delays are God-given opportunities to see and participate in spontaneous God-given moments. The important thing is how you handle delays while not letting them get a hold of you. God is teaching you that He is in control. What might appear to be a delay on our agenda and timeline is really God being right on schedule — His schedule, His timing. Delays are meant to teach us that His timing is perfect. They teach us that our peace is not based on our schedule, but on Him.

So don't let apparent delays rob you of seeing the opportunity God has created right before you. He has something for you to do and experience. Embrace it. Make the most of it. Wherever you are, be there; be in the moment, for that is where God is. When you do, you will see and participate in what He is doing.

Do plan. But know that on the way to your destiny, God will at times insert delays into your schedule. View these as blessings — gifts from Him, surprise moments when He is up to something, allowing you to participate in these opportunities.

John: Stuck in Prison

I, John, your brother and fellow partaker
in the tribulation and kingdom and perseverance
which are in Jesus, was on the island called Patmos
because of the word of God and the testimony of Jesus.
Revelations 1:9

The God-Has-an-Eternal-Purpose Plan
Alias: The Make-the-Most-of-Your-Time Plan

Duration: many year plan[61]
Scripture: Revelation 1:1-10

The apostle John was sentenced to exile on the Island of Patmos for refusing to stop preaching the gospel. It is not known how many years he spent there, or whether he was ever released. But even exile did not stop him. It actually became a place where he received the revelation from the Lord, known as the book of Revelation.

The apostle Paul spent time in prison several times for the same reason John was sent into exile.[62] Yet, while in prison, Paul wrote several letters. Today, these are known as the books of Ephesians, Philippians, Colossians and Philemon.

You may feel stuck. You may feel like you are in exile or prison (or you may be in an actual prison). You may have lost all ability to influence or share like you once did. Perhaps you are going nowhere. But God can and will use you right where you are.

Do not concern yourself with where you are not. This will only distract you from seeing the God-given opportunities right where you are. God is in charge, and He has allowed you to be exactly where you are. He wants to use you there; otherwise He would have made sure you were somewhere else. Though it is not wrong to desire to be somewhere else, do not let this rob you of what God is doing right where you are. This season is a gift from God, allowing you to keep from being distracted by so many other things concerning life.

Make the most of the time right where you are, just like John and Paul did. Spend time praying for others and praising the Lord. Encourage those around you and those at a distance. Ask God for greater revelation of Him and His love. Use this time well.

95

Additional Times When People Waited

- Moses spent forty days on Mount Sinai (Exodus 24:18).
- Moses interceded on behalf of Israel for forty days and nights, waiting for the word of the Lord (Deuteronomy 9:18).
- Joshua marched around Jericho for seven days, waiting for the wall to fall (Joshua 6:1-21).
- Isaiah went barefoot and naked in the wilderness for three years, warning Israel of their future fate if they did not repent (Isaiah 20:3).
- Because of their evil ways, Israel was given over to the Philistines for forty years (Judges 13:1).
- Israel endured the taunting of Goliath for forty days before David slew him (I Samuel 17:16).
- Elijah traveled forty days after eating only one meal, in order to reach Mount Horeb, where God would speak to him (I Kings 19:8).
- Jonah was in the belly of a huge fish for three days, so that he might repent for not doing as the Lord had instructed him, while waiting for the Lord to release him (Jonah 1:17; Matt 12:40).
- The people of Nineveh repented for forty days (Jonah 3:4; 10).
- Ezekiel was instructed by the Lord to lie on his side for 390 days, followed by 40 additional days, portraying to the Israelites the future siege of Jerusalem and Judah (Ezekiel 4:4-6).
- Habakkak waited a lifetime for the Lord to bring about justice (Habakkak 1-3).
- The Lord made Zacharias mute for more than nine months until his son, John the Baptist, was born, because he did not believe the angel who announced the pregnancy in his wife's old age (Luke 1:5-25; 57-80).
- The servants waited for their master's return (Luke 12:35-40).
- Jesus fasted for forty days in the wilderness (Luke 4:1-2).
- After his resurrection, Jesus spent forty days on earth before His ascension, speaking of the kingdom of God (Acts 1:3).

- The disciples waited in the upper room for the Holy Spirit (Acts 1:4-5).
- Elymas the magician was made blind for a season for trying to turn the proconsul from the faith (Acts 13: 8-12).
- Paul spent more than five years in prison (Acts 16:16-18, 21:30-32, 24:26-27).
- We, as believers, are waiting for our son-ship in God to be revealed (Romans 8:18-25).
- Those who lived by faith but did not receive what was promised will receive it in the next life (Hebrews 11:13-16).
- We, as believers, wait for the return of Jesus (Philippians 3:20)!

Application
- When were some times when you waited?
- What did you learn during those times?
- In what ways could your story be an encouragement for others?
- Who is someone with whom you could share your story?

Endnotes

[1] See *Appendix A — Years for Noah to Build the Ark,* for more information.

[2] Genesis 6:15 — the ark was 300 cubits, or 135 meters, which is about 450 feet.

[3] Noah entered the ark in the 600th year of his life, on the seventeenth day of the second month (Genesis 7:11-13). He left the ark on the 27th day of the second month of the following year (Genesis 8:14-15). Therefore, assuming a Jewish lunar calendar of 360 days, he was on the ark for approximately 370 days.

[4] Job 7:3

[5] Abraham was 75 when God first promised him a son (Gen. 12:1-7) . He was 100 when he had his son, Isaac (Gen. 21:5).

[6] Genesis 12:4

[7] *Strong's Concordance*

[8] Also see: Genesis 15:6; Romans 4:3; Galatians 3:6

[9] Genesis 12:10-20

[10] Genesis 20:1-18

[11] Genesis 17:1-4

[12] Sarah was about ten years younger than Abraham (100 - 90 = 10). See Genesis 17:17

[13] Genesis 17:15-17

[14] *Strong's Concordance*

[15] *Strong's Concordance*

[16] Genesis 29:20

[17] Genesis 29:27-30

[18] Hebrews 12:2

[19] Genesis 31:41

[20] Genesis 32:24

[21] *Strong's Concordance*

[22] Joseph was seventeen when he was sold into slavery (Gen. 37:2). He was thirty when he stood before pharaoh (Gen. 41:1).

[23] Acts 7:9-10

[24] Genesis 50:20

[25] Genesis 50:26

[26] Soon after Joseph's death, the Israelites were oppressed as slaves by the Egyptians (Ex. 1:8) for 400 years (Gen. 15:13). When they left Egypt, they took Joseph's bones and wandered in the wilderness for eighty years (40 years times 2). When they got to the Promised Land, Joshua buried Joseph's bones.

[27] Joshua 24:32

[28] Exodus 12:40-41; 15:13; Acts 7:6. To learn more about the years the Israelites spent as slaves in Egypt and the accuracy of the Scriptures on this matter, see *How Long Was the Israelites' Egyptian Bondage?* by Kyle Butt, Apologetics Press, 2002.

[29] Additional insights: when the Israelites first moved to Egypt, this was the Lord's temporary provision for them. They settled in and became accustomed to the place. But when Joseph died, things changed. Their hosts began oppressing them, and eventually, the Israelites became slaves. During this transition, there is no mention of considering an exit plan — like, this would be good time to ask the Lord about heading for the promise land. It was as if they had accepted their fate as slaves. There is not even a record of them crying out to God — not until things got really bad.

During their stay in Egypt, the Israelites were under the rule of a long string of oppressive Egyptian kings. But when the most recent king died, it was as if they finally decided that they had had enough of being slaves. They realized that their circumstances hadn't changed, and therefore, weren't going to get any better. If anything, the next king could be worse!

[30] Numbers 14:33

[31] Joshua 14:10 Caleb was forty when the Israelites spied out the land. He then spent forty years wandering in the desert with his people. He was 85 when he requested his inheritance. 85 - 40 - 40 = 5 years. And he spent some additional time taking possession of his inheritance.

[32] Joshua 1:6,7,9 & 18

[33] In A.D. 70, Titus and the Roman legions destroyed the temple and scattered the Jewish people as slaves among the various provinces of the Roman Empire. On May 14, 1948, Israel was established as an independent and democratic Jewish state.

[34] Acts 7:22-23

[35] Acts 7:22-8:30

[36] Exodus 12:2; Numbers 10:11; plus travel time to the wilderness of Paran (Gen. 12:16) and forty days spying out the land (Num. 13:25).

[37] Acts 6:36

[38] Joshua 14:10

[39] I Samuel 1:7

[40] Acts 13:22

[41] The Bible does not say. But the ancient Jewish historian, Josephus, says that David was ten years old when he was anointed by Samuel to one day become king. David was thirty when he became king over Israel (II Sam. 5:4), though not yet over Judah...

[42] ..It wasn't until seven years after becoming king that David finally became king over Judah as well (II Sam. 5:4-5), thus, finally fulfilling the promise made to him.

[43] II Samuel 12:18

[44] Daniel 4:25

[45] Jeremiah 29:10

[46] Deuteronomy 30

[47] Daniel 10:13

[48] Luke 3:23

[49] John 2:1, 13; Luke 6:1; John 6:4; 12:1; 19:14 — The gospels of John and Luke definitely tell us that at least three Passovers (three years) occurred during Jesus ministry.

[50] Matthew 12:40

[51] Luke 2:29

[52] John 9:20-21 — from birth into adulthood.

[53] John 11:39

[54] A prodigal is a person who spends money in a recklessly extravagant way. (*Oxford Dictionary*)

[55] Galatians 1:17-19

[56] "Paul" was his Greek name, while "Saul" was his Hebrew name (Acts 16:37, 22:25-28).

[57] Acts 9:1-6

[58] 58-63 AD: Acts 22:1-21;28:11

[59] Acts 25:21

[60] Acts 23:11

[61] The Bible does not say how long John was in exile. It is not known whether he died in exile or was released later in life.

[62] Acts 16:16-18, 21:30-32, 24:26-27

The Long Dark Night

So am I made to possess months of misery,
And wearisome nights are appointed to me.
Job 7:3 [ASV]

The Gift of Misery

Several years ago, the Lord spoke to me. I wasn't praying, nor was I thinking of the Lord at that moment. I was walking through the kitchen when it happened. It was not audible. He just interrupted my thoughts and said, "I'm going to give you a gift. ...And that gift is misery." That was it. No details. No explanation. No expiration date.

I didn't know what to say. When I heard Him say, "I'm going to give you a gift," I found myself getting excited. But when He got to the part about "misery," I immediately became ambivalent.

I thought, "How can misery be a gift — especially a gift from the Lord?" Even if it was a gift, I was not sure I wanted it! Yet I had no choice, for the "gift" came immediately.

In the days that followed, I found myself not being able to enjoy anything. Listening to music did nothing for me. I could acknowledge that a sunset was colorful, but I could not feel any beauty from it. Food became a necessary nuisance. I could taste it, but I got no enjoyment from it. It made me feel neither better nor worse. It was not like I hated all these things. I just could not draw any enjoyment from them. Since I was already not sleeping well, this just added to my misery. Life became mundane.

Within six weeks I lost 25 pounds. I changed two belt sizes. My friends even noticed, saying, "Rob, you need to eat more!" Fortunately, about two months into my season of misery, the Lord gave back my enjoyment of food. But everything else remained the same.

As I went about my life, no one seemed to notice that I was miserable, as I tried to keep it to myself. The misery was mostly an internal thing. The few times I shared what I was going through, people did not seem to understand or know what to do. There were times when the misery would subside, and I could have some measure of enjoyment. But eventually it would come back, and any enjoyment I had soon faded. I learned to be thankful for those moments and to make the most of them, knowing they would be infrequent and would not last.

Weeks of misery dragged into months, and months into years. At the writing of this book, I am now three years into this season. When this season began, I did not know how long it would last. I have often had to wrestle with the idea that I may have to live with this condition for the rest of my life. Whenever I have prayed, asking the Lord why I was going through this, He has said it is necessary, and that it is to humble me.

During this season of misery, at times I have struggled with negative thoughts, challenging what the Lord told me and who He is. I have had such thoughts as: "Perhaps this is just my lot in life or that God is punishing me." Or, "God does not love me or has forgotten me." I have had to wrestle against these and other such thoughts.

One day I prayed, asking if the Lord would reassure me about what I thought He had told me previously. Immediately, I was led to read the first chapter of I Samuel. At that moment, I could not recall what the chapter was about, but when I began to read it, the Lord confirmed that what I was going through was from Him!

What stood out for me was that God hallowed Hannah to be miserable, although she had done nothing wrong. The Lord closed her womb so that she was unable to bear children. Year after year she suffered from the ridicule of Peninnah, who mocked her. For years, she cried out to the Lord. She suffered greatly, not only because of Peninnah, but also because of her great desire to have a child. But one day the Lord answered her prayer, and a great prophet was born — Samuel!

Several months after I had this experience, I was at church. The scripture reading for the day was from the seventh chapter of the book of Job. As it was being read, one verse stood out for me, as if someone had used a giant highlighter. It was Job 7:3 (ASV): "So am I made to possess months of misery, and wearisome nights are appointed to me." I was reminded that it was the Lord who had allowed Job to become miserable.

Recently, the Lord has hinted that my season of misery will come to an end soon. But I have learned that my definition of "soon" is not always the same as His.

While I have waited, I have seen some things begin to change in me. I see myself praying in ways I had not done so before, becoming bolder and having greater faith, desiring that I would finish well. I have learned about the meaning of waiting. I am becoming more wanting to wait as I am more aware of my inadequacies, and that I dare not go ahead of the Lord, or without Him.

I have come to a place where, even if the Lord never sets me free from this season of misery, I still want to honor and serve Him. But there is also a tenacity that has grown in me, that I will not stop asking for what I seek from the Lord until He answers, even if it means to the end of the days of my life here on earth.

Not all seasons the Lord takes us through are seasons of misery. He may not require that you go through such a season. If it is required of you, it is because it is necessary for what He has for you. Be reassured — He loves you and is committed to you. He has great plans and purposes, which include you. He is committed to making you more like Jesus.

Think of it this way as to why the Lord takes you through difficult seasons of any kind. If you ever sang the song, "Make me like you, Lord," the Lord is answering your prayer! If you are like me, you find yourself saying, "Yes, make me like You, Lord. But can You do it in another way?!"

Misery

Whether it is misery, suffering or affliction, we all experience these to various degrees in our lives. Sometimes these are caused by others, or we may bring them on ourselves. Regardless, the Lord will use them to shape and prepare us for His purposes. When the Lord does this, it is to discipline us and to bring about change. Here are some verses that speak of this very thing:

> Make us glad according to the days You have afflicted us, and the years we have seen evil (Psalm 90:15).

> I know, O LORD, that Your judgments are righteous, and that in faithfulness You have afflicted me (Psalm 119:75).

Before I was afflicted I went astray, but now I keep Your word (Psalm 119:67).

It is good for me that I was afflicted, that I may learn Your statutes (Psalm 119:71).

For they [our fathers] disciplined us for a short time as seemed best to them, but He disciplines us for our good, so that we may share His holiness (Hebrews 11:10).

Thoughts on Misery

Misery is experiencing ongoing suffering with little or no relief in sight.

It motivates you to change what you can, and then to cry out for change of that which you cannot.

Misery can be a small thing, but if it is persistent over long periods of time, it eventually begins to wear you down. It can be the summation of a lot of little things chipping away at your strength, abilities and dreams. It is like a constant smoldering that burns ever so slowly, but continuously. It can seem like it never lets up.

Some of the most difficult sufferings are those hidden from everyone else's view. Yet, they are very real to the person who is suffering.

Yielding to your state of misery only reinforces negative beliefs such as: "It's never going to get better," "There is nothing you can do about it." and, "It's bound to get worse." But when you overcome misery by enduring and persevering, you prove these statements wrong!

Misery exists in two forms. There is misery that happens to us, and there is misery that stems from our beliefs and our perceptions of our circumstances. Misery is something that can be imposed upon us, and it is something we can impose upon ourselves. While in some instances we may not have asked for it, we definitely have the choice whether or not to let it control us. This is the very thing we are to learn while in the midst of misery — that though we are in a miserable situation, we do not need to be miserable.

The Purpose of Misery

God uses misery in our lives for many reasons. Here are just a few:

Misery challenges us to no longer just know *about* God, but to know *Him*. It awakens our soul to the ways we are only giving lip service to God, and causes us to engage in relationship with Him.

Waiting in the midst of misery allows us to become so dissatisfied that nothing else matters than that for which we are waiting.

It is an opportunity to realize what matters most in life, and to choose that, while letting go of things that don't really matter. In letting go of things we hold so tightly, we learn the reality that they were the very things that were keeping us from experiencing peace and freedom in the first place. And in many instances, they were the things that were adding to our misery.

Misery is a means to put to death our flesh (I Peter 4:1), to free us from those things which hinder us from being all we can be for God.

A season of misery is an opportunity to allow us to turn our misery into longsuffering. Longsuffering is patience in the midst of pain or suffering. It is choosing to wait as you bear whatever afflictions that have come your way, knowing that God is in charge and that He has a greater purpose in store. The Lord is longsuffering toward us. He chooses to suffer as He waits for us to repent from our sinful ways. This character in Himself, He is forming in you.

Misery allows us the privilege to enter into the fellowship of Christ's sufferings (Philippians 3:10). It lets us get just a small glimpse of what Christ went through on the cross for us out of His great love. It allows us to see just how momentary and small our afflictions truly are in light of His sufferings and how great the glory is that is to come(I Corinthians 4:17).

It is the opportunity for head knowledge to become head knowledge, transforming us.

What to Do in the Midst of Misery

Rise up in spite of the misery. Get to the point where you can continue on and go about your day, despite the presence of misery in your life. No longer let it dictate who you are and what you will do and not do on any given day. Though misery greets you when you wake up in the morning, choose to no longer let it influence your day. Though it keeps you up all night, choose to not let your heart be troubled. Though it continues to yell in your ear to give up, tune it out. Instead, turn toward the Lord, seeking Him while you wait.

The Long Dark Night

We all go through various challenging seasons. Some people have more of them than others. Some of these trying times are longer than others. And some are harder. The Lord will take some people through periods of waiting that are longer and more intense than others. These are called: "Long Dark Nights."

You do not have to have the Lord speak to you in order to know you are in the Long Dark Night. You will know simply because you are in it. There is no particular duration to the Long Dark Night. It is as long as the Lord assigns it to be

The Long Dark Night can be likened to an endless night of sleeplessness. Though you are so exhausted and stressed, no matter what you do, you can't get any sleep. You toss and turn all night long. Even if you are able to get to sleep, it is short-lived and full of bad dreams. Darkness is all around you. The night seems to never end. When morning comes, you are still very tired, and the whole thing repeats itself the very next night. This is what my gift-of-misery is like. Perhaps you can relate.

The Long Dark Night is long because it seems like it will never end, as if it will always be part of your life. It is referred to as dark because of its obscurity and the unknown — you are not able to see what is going on, where you are going, or why it is happening. Spiritually, you feel as if you are in the dark. It is night because you wonder where God has gone, and any light you may have had before is gone or is now only a flicker.

The Long Dark Night is often referred to as a time in the desert or wilderness. David refers to his Long Dark Night as "the valley of the shadow of death" (Psalm 23:4). Moses apparently had no name for his forty-year experience in the desert as a shepherd. But he did refer to his forty-year wandering with the Israelites as days of affliction and years of trouble (Psalm 90:15). Hannah, described her misery as being "oppressed of spirit" (I Samuel 1:14). Some friends of mine call their Long Dark Night their "fiery trial" (I Peter 4:12).

But with each one, their Long Dark Night did come to end. At the end of his, David wrote many Psalms of praise to God. Moses wrote a song, glorifying the Lord (Deuteronomy 32). Hannah rejoiced greatly with much praise to God (I Samuel 2).

At the end of his years of suffering, Joseph referred to his Long Dark Night as a time that his brothers "...meant...for evil but God meant...for good" (Genesis 50:20). And as an expression of his gratitude and praise to the Lord, Joseph gave very special names to his two sons, Manasseh and Ephraim. Manasseh means, "God has made me forget all my trouble and all my father's household" (Genesis 41:60). Ephraim means, "God has made me fruitful in the land of my affliction" (vs. 61).

Concerning your Long Dark Night, my prayer for you is that the Lord will, as it says in Psalm 90:15, "...make us glad according to the days You have afflicted us, and the years we have seen evil."

In the 1600's, St. John of the Cross wrote of his experience of the Long Dark Night in his book titled, *Dark Night of the Soul*.[3] The following are some insights he gleaned from his experience.

During the Long Dark Night, the desire to pray or read the Bible is gone. Seeking the Lord feels dry, empty and rehearsed. You no longer feel His presence. The enjoyment of spending time with other Christians is gone. All these things feel like work. There is no joy in them, nor is there any anticipation of joy. It makes you tired just thinking about doing any of these things.

The Long Dark Night is not because of caused by of some sin or failure in your life. You are in it because you are faithfully following Christ — even though in the midst of it you see no success.

You are in it because God does love you — even though at this moment His love seems to be far away, and almost a forgotten memory.

You are in it because you are on the right path. You have not taken a wrong turn. The path of the Long Dark Night is narrow, and few take it. Or, in your case, somehow you found yourself on it and don't know how to get off of it. And will you ever? If you feel this way, you are on the path of the Long Dark Night.

You are on it because the Lord has chosen you. He has not forgotten you.

---

[3] See the book, *Dark Night of the Soul*, by St. John of the Cross.

The Long Dark Night is meant to bring you to a place where your fear of the Lord is no longer expressed in words like, "Oh no, what if He uncovers my sin?!" Rather, you will find yourself saying, "I am undone. I know I have nothing to hide!" You run toward God instead of away from Him.

During the Long Dark Night you will learn that just because you do not feel the Lord's presence this does not mean He is not present. He is always present: "I will never leave nor forsake you" (Deuteronomy 31:6). Instead, He is teaching you to know His presence in ways greater than feeling His presence. Even though it feels like He doesn't hear you, you come to know that He does hear you. even though it appears that He is doing nothing, you begin to know in your spirit that He is. More importantly, the Lord is teaching you to be satisfied with Him with or without spiritual gifts and experiences — to be simply satisfied with Jesus. And once this satisfaction has been formed in you, God can trust you with more gifts and more experiences than before.

The Purpose of the Long Dark Night

Though your Long Dark Night may or may not be like mine, the purpose is the same.

To break your confidence in your own capacity and abilities. The Lord brings you to a point where, though you have certain strengths and talents, your reliance is not on these things, but on Him.

To make you aware of the depth of your sin. This is not to shame you, but to bring you to complete surrender and reliance on Him as Lord and Savior.

To put to death whatever needs to be dealt with. It may be different for you than for me. But the end result is the same — death to self.

To remove the dross of self-centeredness and self-serving.

To remove the worst in you and bring out the best of Him in and through you.

To call forth perseverance and surrender.

To bring you to a point where your life no longer matters to you, but living for Him does.

To keep you from becoming a needless casualty of war.[4] God is preparing you for something important. What He is doing now in you will enable you to accomplish and finish what He has for you to do.

Why does the Lord do all this?

Because the best thing for you to be is humble.

Because, for whatever He has planned for you, He needs an instrument for His service whose sin and self do not get in the way.

Because He wants what you want — a closer relationship with Him!

Things not to do while in the Long Dark Night:
- Do not try to get out of it.
- Do not curse God.
- Do not quit. Every time you fall down, get back up.

While prayer will help you get through the Long Dark Night, it will not get you out of it. It is something you must go through and complete. Nor can you go around it. And the Long Dark Night is not something that can be prayed away. There are no inner healing issues that must be resolved in order for you to be set free from this season. Though you might experience healing in the midst of it, the Long Dark Night is not something that must or can be healed. If the Lord were to take you out of it too soon, you would only have to start all over again.

God does not take you through the Long Dark Night because He is punishing you. He is taking you through it because He loves you and has a special purpose for you. Every son He loves He disciplines. Discipline is an investment for your good, punishment is retribution for a wrong you have done. You are in the Long Dark Night because you have done something right — you have refused to settle for something less in your relationship with God.

What to Do While in the Long Dark Night
- Continue to seek the Lord while you wait.
- Be faithful, and trust in Him.

---

[4] See the book, *Needless Casualties of War*, by John Paul Jackson.

- Whatever you are doing, do your best, and make the most of it.
- Choose to serve and honor the Lord, no matter what.

Lessons to Be Learned

During my time in the Long Dark Night, the Lord has taught me many things. Most importantly, these things have gone from being just knowledge to being written in my heart. That is what He has for you, as well.

Initially, while in the Long Dark Night you may feel like you are not learning anything. You might find yourself questioning even what you thought you knew. You might even think you are going backward. Know that this is normal. It is usually toward the end of the Long Dark Night, or when it is over, that you discover what you have learned and what has transpired in your heart. This is when you realize that the Long Dark Night has indeed been a gift. Before this realization, it will not seem like a gift at all.

So that you might be encouraged, here are few examples of just some of the things I have learned during my Long Dark Night —the "gift of misery."

Where Do You Abide?

During my Long Dark Night, the Lord has revealed to me ways I have not abided in Him. Rather, I have abided in other things. Jesus said, "Abide in Me, and I in you" (John 15:4). "Abide in My love" (John 15:9). How does one do this?

We have a choice of that in which we will abide. We all abide in something. Abiding means: to dwell, to take refuge in. When things are going bad, in what do you choose to take refuge? When your circumstances are pressing you to become anxious, do you choose to be worried or to be patient? When someone does you wrong and you are tempted to retaliate, do you choose to get even or to do good? Do you abide in imaginary arguments with those who have offended you? Or, do you choose forgiveness? When all is falling apart around you, do you choose to be afraid, or do you abide in peace? The Long Dark Night will teach you that no matter how dark and hopeless it may seem, you can abide in God's love. Though despair may be all around you, you do not have to despair. You can abide in hope and peace.

When someone offends you or calls you a name, do you choose to abide in the offense, or do you choose to abide in how the Lord sees you?

Some of us abide in old things from our past. We abide in shame and guilt, despite knowing that the Lord has forgiven us. Or, we abide in labels and negative statements others have spoken over or about us.

When everything around you gives reason to feel anxious, know that Jesus is not anxious. When others are impatient, Jesus is not. In the boat in the midst of the storm, Jesus took a nap. He was abiding in the Father. Because His Father was not bothered or fearful, neither was He. He did not abide in the storm, by allowing it to tell Him how he should respond. The key is to find what Jesus is doing in the midst of your storm, and to do what He is doing. This is abiding in Jesus.

When you think of abiding in Jesus, remember the fruit of the Spirit: love, joy, peace, patience, kindness, goodness, faithfulness, gentleness, and self-control (Galatians 5:22-23). That's where Jesus will be dwelling. And that is where you and I should be.

During times when I have felt miserable, my tendency has been to dwell on the misery — to whine, to believe the worst, to doubt, etc. But the Lord has been training me to choose not to dwell in the misery, despite its oppressiveness. I have learned that I have a choice — either to give into the misery or to act in way that is contradictory to my misery. I either abide in the misery or I abide in the Lord.

The other day as I woke up, I was tempted to still feel guilty for something I had done wrong, even though I had confessed it as sin. The Lord reminded me that His mercies are new every morning (Lamentations 3:22-23). I had a choice to make. He had done His part: to forgive. My part was to choose to embrace His incredible love, no matter how I felt. No matter how many times I have failed, He forgives. So I chose that morning to abide in His love, not in guilt. And it made a huge difference!

Imagine a row of houses. On one of the houses there is a sign that reads: "Jesus." Under it is a list of the fruits of the Spirit. On the other side of the street are houses representing the deeds of the flesh (Galatians 5:19-21). When circumstances go bad, which house do you run to? Which do you choose to dwell in? Do you allow your choices to be dictated by circumstances or people, and thus, run into the house that reflects that experience? Or, do you choose to dwell where Jesus dwells?

> The name of the LORD is a strong tower;
> The righteous runs into it and is safe.
> Proverbs 18:10

The Long Dark Night will reveal those wrong places you dwell when things get bad. And if you allow it, it will eventually teach you that you can dwell in the Lord, despite how bad it gets.

To No Longer Settle for Less

During my Long Dark Night, the Lord revealed how I, as well as some of my ancestors, had settled for less in life. We had accepted complacency and passivity as contentment. We had allowed the enemy to slowly redefine love, life, passion, parenting, bonding, God, and more. The meaning of these blessings became slowly watered-down with each generation, and no one questioned what was happening. No one rose up and said, "We have been losing ground. We've got to do something about it. There is something wrong with us. Let's seek the Lord for help!" Instead, they settled for each incremental change. They settled for less. And they went numb to the price they were paying.

The Long Dark Night woke me up to this pattern in my family-line. It allowed me to realize and feel the loss that occurred due to our settling for less. Thus, it brought me to a place where I began to cry out to God to undo what had been done for generations. As far as I know, I am the first to take this step.

How about you? Are you willing to be the one to make a difference and put an end to settling for less, or whatever is the stronghold in your family line? As needed, the Long Dark Night will reveal those areas that need to be addressed.

Thy Will Be Done

Too often I have asked the Lord for mercy, only so I could avoid the consequences of my actions. So many times, He has been merciful and gracious, despite what I did.

The Long Dark Night will bring you to a place where you no longer care about avoiding consequences. Rather, you will long for the Lord to change you. It will bring you to a place where you no longer fight the process the Lord is taking you through. You will submit to Him, saying, "Thy will be done."

Overcome Misery

The Long Dark Night will teach you that despite your miserable situation, you don't have to choose to be miserable. It will bring you to a place where what you thought was impossible is actually possible — you don't have to be ruled by your misery.

Significance

Significance is knowing that you are important and valued, and that you matter. During the Long Dark Night you feel that your life is going nowhere. You will feel left behind and forgotten while others move ahead. All that you have done may now seem gone. Perhaps many of your accomplishments and intended goals have amounted to nothing. It is in the midst of this that the source of your sense of significance will be confronted. For is your significance in your accomplishments, abilities and the praise of men — or is it in the Lord?

This is exactly what my time during the Long Dark Night has revealed to me. The most difficult part was not being able to secure my sense of significance, especially since things I had based it on, other than the Lord, were no longer available. Worse was not knowing how to get free from still desiring those erroneous ways.

Fortunately, if you let it, the Long Dark Night will bring you to a place where, no matter what, your sense of significance is in the Lord and what He thinks of you. This truth will begin to rise up within you, to the point where, even if you do great things, you want nothing more than for your significance to be in Him.

What Really Matters Most

A few days ago, I found out that I am going to be laid-off at the end of the month. I was surprised by my response! I didn't get depressed like I normally would have in the past. I didn't get angry, either. Yes, I was disappointed, but I had peace.

What I realized is that my experience during the Long Dark Night has prioritized what really matters most to me: to know the Lord, and to wait on Him. Yes, I would rather have my job and not have to go looking for another one. But, compared to what now really matters to me, my job situation did not even compare. It simply became something I have to attend to and trust God to provide as I do my part.

There are more lessons I have learned during my Long Dark Night, and these are just a few. Your Long Dark Night may or may not be like mine, but there is a purpose for it, and you will learn many lessons as well that will change you and set you free.

Even if...

Many years ago, I went through a season when I was not sure if I was saved. Looking back, I can't recall any events that brought this about. During that time, despite that I knew what is stated in the Bible, I could not shake feelings of doubt and uncertainty. I often felt discouraged in my attempts to resist them. I began to feel insecure about my future. And I had no idea if I would ever be freed from this way of thinking. All I could do was resist it and believe the truth, in spite of how I felt.

Many months later, for no apparent reason, the feelings of doubt and uncertainty finally lifted. During that difficult experience, I had no idea why I was going through it. Yet, after it was over, I realized something. Toward the end of that period, a new way of thinking had begun to enter my heart. I found myself concluding: that even if I was not saved or could not know for sure if I was, God is still worthy to be honored and served. The emphasis became more about Him and less about me. It was soon after this truth had entered my heart that the struggle had lifted off of me.

The Long Dark Night will confront erroneous strongholds in your heart that limit your commitment to the Lord. It will bring you to a place where all that matters is Him despite whatever you don't understand. Peace comes when these things no longer get in the way of your relationship with Him.

So here is something I would challenge you to think about. Would you serve and honor our Lord Jesus Christ, even if:

... you never knew for sure if you were saved?

...you lost your health, job, money, and possessions?

...you saw the wicked prosper and the righteous oppressed?

...you had to suffer the loss of a loved one or identify with a loved one's suffering?

...life did not go your way?

...the Lord never answered your prayers or never fulfilled His promises in this life?

...He never fulfilled your dreams, or He took them away?

...He blessed others and not you?

I will let you in on something: God is worthy to be served and honored, no matter what.

When the Lord takes us through the Long Dark Night, it changes us. As we wait, we will eventually come to a place where there is nothing and no one we want to wait upon, other than Him. He becomes the only One who is worth waiting for. All previous options become no options at all. It is Him or nothing. This is not unlike the time when Jesus asked the disciples, "You do not want to go away also, do you?" and Peter replied, "Lord, to whom shall we go? You have words of eternal life. We have believed and have come to know that You are the Holy One of God" (John 6:67-68). It is at this point that we are willing to wait for Him no matter what, even if it takes a lifetime.

He is worth the wait!

Know that in your Long Dark Night, God is working various things into you, and other things out of you. Remember, you are not alone. Others have gone through, or are going through, similar things. God is not done with you yet.

For it is God who is at work in you,
both to will and to work for His good pleasure.
Philippians 2:13

Application

- Has there been a time you went through a Long Dark Night? How do you know?
- What are some of the things the Lord taught (or is teaching) you during the Long Dark Night?
- What were some of the hardest things you experienced during that time?
- What promises has He made to you, despite what you went through or are going through?
- Spend time renewing your commitment to Him.
- Who is someone you could be able to share with about what you have gone, or are going, through?
- Knowing what you know now, is there someone you know who is going through the Long Dark Night? What are some ways you could be an encouragement and support for them?

So What's in Your Prayer?

Ask, and it will be given to you;
Seek, and you will find;
Knock, and it will be opened to you.
Matthew 7:7

Tom's Prayer

When my son-in-law, Tom, was nineteen, he decided he wanted to join the US Coast Guard. Tom loves helping people, and he knew this would be a great career and a good fit for him. Yet, upon talking to a recruiter, Tom discovered that applicants with certain physical conditions are often denied enlistment. This was initially discouraging for Tom, because of his condition.

As a teenager, Tom had been a competitive gymnast, which had made him very physically fit. Unfortunately, he had damaged his shoulders. Despite enduring four surgeries, he was still left with a limited range of arm motion above his head. When he shared about this with the recruiter, he was told that it was unlikely he would make it through the application process.

Despite this possibility, Tom decided to persevere and apply anyway, then wait and see how far in the application process he could go. He committed this by faith in prayer to the Lord, trusting in Him.

The application process required that Tom take a physical. Although he knew it might cost him his acceptance, he decided to be upfront about his condition. He chose to trust the Lord and not manipulate the situation by hiding it. To his amazement, he passed his physical! Unfortunately, at the same time, he discovered that he was color blind. Although this would not prevent him from being accepted, it closed the door to various jobs he wanted within the Coast Guard. Yet, he decided that if God had brought him this far, he would continue to persevere and trust Him with this issue as well.

Then a delay occurred. Tom was told that there weren't any openings and that it could be a year or more before any would become available. There was even a possibility that he might never get in. Being determined and willing to wait as long as took, he decided he would persevere by continuing to call the recruiting office every two weeks. Each time, he asked if there were any openings, and each time, he received the same answer as before. It sounded like he would be forever put off. But, rather than give-up, he decided to trust the Lord. For the next year and half, every two weeks he called the recruiting office. Then, one day, it all paid off. He got accepted!

At age 23, Tom successfully completed boot camp and was assigned a post. There, he was given another test for color blindness. This time he passed! This opened up opportunities he was previously told were not available to him.

What is encouraging about Tom's story is that he did not give-up. He pursued what was on his heart. He persisted despite apparent obstacles, and trusted the Lord while he waited. He was determined to not let any roadblocks prevent him from moving forward. While waiting, he did what he could do. He became the best employee he could at whatever job he had at the time. He also encouraged and helped others, spent time with family and friends, and kept himself physically fit. As a result, God made things happen for him, despite his physical conditions and any delays. In the end, it was worth all the effort and waiting!

Prayers

For most of us, our prayer life is filled with short-term prayers about our immediate daily needs or those of others. These are important prayers. We need to ask God to bless our day, and to give us wisdom or courage as we need it. We need to ask Him to bless and help our children as they go to school or face a challenge, to help us with an immediate need, or to assist us in finding our keys or something else we have lost.

But then, there are long-term prayers. These are the ones that don't get answered right away. These are the ones that require perseverance and persistence. These are the ones that will stretch our faith, while allowing us the opportunity to exercise faith despite our situation.

Perhaps we know of someone who does not know the Lord or has strayed from Him. We may have a friend who is still out of work or is struggling with a long-term illness or injury. I know of someone who has been waiting for years to go to school but has been prevented thus far.

If one is up to the challenge, these and other such situations require long-term prayer.

Concerning long-term prayers, how long should one pray? As long as it takes!

Ask, Seek, Knock

In Matthew 7:7, the words, "ask," "seek," and "knock" all have one thing in common. In the Greek, they are all in the present active imperative. This means they are in the present and the ongoing tense at the same time. So, to ask is not to ask just once. It is to ask and keep on asking. "Seek" means to seek and keep on seeking. "Knock" means to knock and keep on knocking. So when it comes to praying, we are to pray and to keep on praying.

In the verses that follow Matthew 7:7, Jesus illustrates how these things are to be done. He speaks of a man who did not allow annoying his neighbor stop him from asking for what he needed. He did not let having his request denied stop him from asking again and again. This is what God wants us to do — to be persistent. He wants us to keep pressing Him with our requests. This is not to wear us out, but to work something in us.

What is key here is not so much the asking, but the persistence in asking. Anyone can ask. But how many ask and continue to ask?

The process of continuing to ask is very important. This separates the sprinters from the long-distance runners. If you are not a long-distance runner yet, it will make you into one. It will refine you — it will remove any remnant of hesitancy and passivity. If you allow it, it will build tenacity into you. It will bring you more and more into a place where nothing else matters than continuing to ask, no matter what.

The process of persistence will refine your prayer. Over a long period of time, your prayer will become more focused on what matters most.

It is like going on a long trek with a loaded backpack. As you go, you discover what it is that you really need in your pack — what is your bare minimum. So you lighten the load and carry only what you really need. Thus, the trek becomes more bearable as you head toward your destination.

As I mentioned in a previous chapter, one of the reasons the Lord has taken me through such long times of persisting has been to break the pattern in my family-line of settling for less. What better way than to persist in prayer?

When Hannah asked God for a child, it was not because He told her to ask. Rather, she did this on her own accord. It was the one thing that mattered most to her. She persisted in prayer, not settling for less, until she got what she desired (I Samuel 1).

Jabez did not wait for some sign from the Lord that he should ask for what he desired most of all — to be delivered from his past pain. He chose to not settle for his past and merely getting by. Instead, he kept asking the Lord until He finally honored his prayer (I Chronicles 4:9-10).

Daniel's desire was that the Lord would forgive the iniquities of his nation and deliver them from captivity (Daniel 9). His custom to pray as much as he did was not something the Lord told him to do. Rather, it was out of what his own longing.

So here is my challenge to you: What would you ask for, as your long-term prayer? What would you continue to seek the Lord for, despite apparent obstacles, delays and challenges? What closed doors would you persist in knocking upon until they open? What is on your heart that you would be willing to pray for — no matter how long it takes, no matter how long you must wait?

Go for it!

Application

- What would your most important prayer be?
- What do you want most, that only God can make happen?
- What would keep you from persisting in prayer for what you want?
- What would be the amazing benefits if the Lord answered your prayer?
- Perhaps there was a time when you pursued God in prayer, but you quit. Ask the Lord to help you as you choose to get back in there. And in the midst of your waiting, make the most your time and continue...

    ...asking, seeking and knocking!

How to Become a Christian

If you desire to become a Christian, pray the following prayer to Jesus.

"Jesus, I acknowledge that I am a sinner and that You died for my sins. I receive You as my Lord and Savior. Come into my life. I ask that you fill me with your Holy Spirit and that You direct me in all that I do."

Congratulations! You are now God's child.

Now that you have become a Christian, do the following:
- Find another Christian, and tell him/her what you did today!
- Get involved in a local church, especially one that has small home-groups that meet during the week for Bible study and prayer.
- Begin reading the Bible. I encourage you to begin in the New Testament, starting with book of John.
- Spend time with Jesus in prayer. He has loves spending time with you!

www.ingramcontent.com/pod-product-compliance
Lightning Source LLC
Chambersburg PA
CBHW060313050426
42448CB00009B/1809